CALIFORNIA CUISINE

CARMEL BERMAN REINGOLD

AVON
PUBLISHERS OF BARD, CAMELOT, DISCUS AND FLARE BOOKS

CALIFORNIA CUISINE is an original publication of Avon Books. This work has never before appeared in book form.

AVON BOOKS
A division of
The Hearst Corporation
959 Eighth Avenue
New York, New York 10019

Book design by Peter Bender

Library of Congress Cataloging in Publication Data

Reingold, Carmel Berman.
    California cuisine.

    Includes index.
    1. Cookery, American—California. 2. Wine and winemaking—California. 3. Restaurants, lunch rooms, etc.—California. I. Title.
TX715.R41127   1983   641.59794   82–90527
ISBN 0–380–82156–7

First Avon Printing, February, 1983

Printed in the U. S. A.

DON   10 9 8 7 6 5 4 3 2 1

CALIFORNIA CUISINE

Contents

1   California: Life Style and Food Style   1
2   Those Entertaining Californians   7
3   To Begin With: Inventive Appetizers   13
4   For a Different Brunch   35
5   A Sampling of Soups   45
6   A Big Garden Called California: Vegetables and Salads   53
7   The California Fish Story: On the Light Side, Fish
    and Shellfish   73
8   Meats and Poultry: Prepared in New, Ethnic, Classic
    and Traditional Ways   97
9   Breads, Quiches, Calzone and Burritos   123
10 Special Touches: Sauces, Relishes and Butters   131
11 Desserts in Abundance: Light or Rich   141
12 Guide to California Wines   165
13 As California Goes . . .   173

    Sources of Ingredients   176
    Index   179

California: 1
Life Style and
Food Style

Sophie Porter

For years, as a New Yorker, I thought that American styles and trends started in the East. I did understand that we were influenced by Europe, but I was always surprised when traveling in Europe to be told that my clothes, my walk, my outgoing attitude made me typically American.

In recent years, however, I became aware of changes in American life style that chipped away at my provincial attitude. Clothes, for example: everyone seemed to be dressing more casually. And at the same time, everyone was quite serious about health and exercise. More people were joining gyms and health spas and embarking on serious programs of self-maintenance.

And then there were the observable changing tastes in food and drink. Once dedicated Scotch and whiskey drinkers were now ordering white wine or drinks made with vodka. French *haute cuisine* was still considered great, but great in an old-fashioned, period-piece way. Northern Italian cuisine was popular, but pasta and veal dishes could not be served seven days a week.

One day I took a closer look at the clothes in my closet and at the food in my kitchen. I saw many items labeled "Made in California" and "Grown in California."

Food writers whose articles appeared in newspapers and magazines were the first to write about California food styles, and they used words like *eclectic* and *wholesome,* and frequently combined *wholesome* with *hedonistic* in the same sentence. Friends came back to New York from trips West and raved about special restaurants they had found in Berkeley or in the Napa Valley.

What was going on? This past year I decided to find out for myself, and I made the journey that so many Americans had made before me; I went West—to California. During my visit I learned that California is not just a state, it is also a state of mind, and a state of mind that influences the rest of our country.

I saw that Californians, both native and adopted, are true to their historic heritage. California has always been the place for the adventurous. Years ago people went there to hunt for gold and to search for new frontiers. Today, Americans from other states still look towards California. What is the magic they hope to find there? Sunshine, warmth, a more relaxed way of looking at life, a certain hedonism, a willingness to ignore the problems of the rest of the world—that's the lure of Southern California. The North offers San Francisco, and the dream of big city chic and sophistication in a small city environment.

Americans from the rest of the country and immigrants from the Far East and Europe quickly subscribe to California's frontier spirit, an interesting combination of personal daring and social conservatism.

I can do anything. I can make it. And if I can, so can you.

It's no wonder that this rugged individualism has resulted in the election of two such diverse personalities as Ronald Reagan and Jerry Brown as governors of the state.

Are personalities and personal life styles reflected in the way a people cook and eat? Absolutely. As General de Gaulle said, "How can you govern a nation whose people eat four hundred different kinds of cheese?"

The English have traditionally cared more for what they wear to dinner than what they eat when they get there, while the Italians concentrate on using the finest ingredients, in clothing as well as in food, and in keeping the preparations comparatively simple.

And what about us? It would seem that America is too large, too heterogeneous to be tethered to one way of thinking or one way of cooking. But if there is any place that has taken a variety of experiences and life styles and synthesized them into something uniquely its own, it is California.

California offers a spirited combination of the daring of the first explorers, the bravery of the pioneers, Far Eastern and Mexican cultures, and the regional attitudes of other Americans. All this is blended together with Western verve and creativity, and the result is very Californian. In a short time this mix acquires form and substance and is translated into trends which then move cross-country to become quintessentially American.

This movement of ideas from West to East has been going on for years. According to wine and liquor manufacturers who track these matters, the taste for "white and light" drinks, meaning vodka and white wine, started in California. Many people around the country are now enrolled in courses of instruction on the art of judging and tasting wine; the courses were first given in California.

Manufacturers of major cooking appliances have long told me that food processors and convection ovens were first popular in California. Chuck Williams, whose elegant Williams-Sonoma Catalog for Cooks is mailed around the country, started in California; he now has four shops there specializing in the finest tabletop ware and kitchenware. Often, when plans are made to open similar stores in other states, smart entrepreneurs visit the San Francisco or Beverly Hills branch of Williams-Sonoma to see how it is done.

Recently, there has been a proliferation of Mexican-style food in supermarkets, as well as Mexican fast-food restaurants, and this, too, is another example of California influence.

Barbecues, hot tubs, jacuzzis—they all got their start in California.

Sportswear, which seems to be all that most people wear whether they're picnicking or going to the theatre, started in California. Designers like

Helga Howie, Rudy Gernreich, and Bob Mackie and manufacturers such as Cole and Esprit create in California and go on to influence the rest of the country.

Jogging is now a national pastime, but it first became popular in California, as did tennis. And there are many people who neither jog nor play tennis but who wear jogging shorts and warm-up suits just for fun, a very California outlook.

Californians are willing to spend their money on pleasure, and to them, pleasure means doing rather than observing. What starts out as fun may end up as big business. Vineyards are one of the new, "in" investments. And this doesn't mean a big vineyard like the one owned by the Gallo Brothers, but a smaller vineyard such as the one started by the Trefethen family. The Trefethens originally put a few acres into wine grapes for their own pleasure, and then went on to develop a wine company that took honors at a Paris wine tasting.

Easterners, viewing the success of the small California vineyards, are now trying to do likewise, and small vineyards are proliferating in upper New York State as well as in the potato country of Eastern Long Island.

Did the Western look come from Texas? It came from farther west than that. That ubiquitous cowboy hat didn't really take off until after it was popularized by Californians who have now gone into ranching and horse breeding.

Movie producer Ray Stark, actress Bo Derek and her husband, John, and the Ronald Reagans all have ranches in the Santa Ynez valley, as does Brooks Firestone, who has both a cattle ranch and a winery. Not everyone can afford the cost of feed for a stable of horses, but everyone can afford a Western hat.

With the increase in physical activity has come the increase in self-maintenance. Thin, slim, tanned, healthy, that's the California look, and it's the look the rest of the country wants. Why else the silly craze for tanning salons in not-so-sunny Chicago and New York, and the commercials extolling the sexy possibilities of being "California slim"?

All around the country people are flocking to health spas and gyms. They are consulting experts who create individually planned exercise programs. It's all in emulation of the healthy, West Coast look, but to look like a Californian one must eat like a Californian. *You are what you eat* is a cliché, but it is also true. *Natural* is a word heard a lot in California, as is *fresh*, as are *wholesome* and *new* and *light*. One or more of these concepts is used in what is now referred to as California Cuisine, and will soon become the New American Cuisine.

Californians have their own, pleasurable way of interpretation. For example, *artificial* is out, and many Californians insist that they must have *real*, grain-fed chickens—no hormones, please. However, once they have that natural and wholesome chicken they will often serve it with a rich *crème fraîche* sauce, hence the combination of wholesome and hedonistic. Cheese cakes must be made with cream cheese that is free of additive gums. No one is claiming that the cheese cakes are low in calories, but at least they are *pure* and *wholesome*.

If meat and fish are grilled without fats of any kind, they are frequently garnished with flavored butters or sauces. A vegetarian restaurant in California is expected to be as elegant as any other fine food establishment, and while you may have a brochette of tofu and vegetables as a main course, you can follow it with a chocolate mousse pie or almond-raspberry tart for dessert.

The serious chefs of California were constantly telling me that what they are doing is a version of the regional cuisine so familiar in France.

"We just use what we have," I heard more than once.

But in France one region may have fresh goose livers and truffles, while another provides oysters. Chickens are a speciality in one corner of the country, duck in another, and fruits and vegetables in a third. The difference between California regional cuisine and the regional cuisine of France is that in California they start out with just about everything. And enjoying such bounty, they can use it with a lavish hand, creating food combinations that have not as yet been tried elsewhere.

California cuisine is definitely aided by California's agriculture: artichokes, avocados, figs, dates, and nuts, citrus fruits, lettuce and tomatoes, nectarines and plums, olives, grapes for eating and grapes for wine-making, all and more can be found in the abundance that is California.

When farmers came to California in the 19th century from rocky New England soil, and frozen, mid-Western prairies, they were looking for gold. When they didn't find it, they returned to farming and created the cornucopia that is California today, with more than 900,000 acres under cultivation.

Fruits and vegetables grow easily; their abundance lowers the price, encouraging chefs to be more daring, more innovative. They can afford to take chances, make mistakes, try combinations that might work marvelously or might not work at all.

If the usual grows in abundance, so does the unusual. Mexicans like jicama, a vegetable that looks like a turnip, but has a far sweeter crunch. Jicama is now grown in California, as are Jerusalem artichokes, which Californians call sunchokes. If garlic is great, Elephant Garlic is even greater, and if kiwi fruit can be grown in New Zealand, why can't it be grown in California? It can, and it is, as are pistachios. Americans used to munch on Iranian pistachios; they're munching more happily now on home-grown nuts.

Harvests from the valleys of California, Imperial and Sonoma, Napa and San Jose, Salinas and San Joaquin—and harvests, too, from the waters of California, offering Petrale sole, Pacific snapper, Bay shrimp, and much more—all this is easily available. The abundance and variety influence the creators of California cuisine.

Where can these innovators be found? Some of them are hard at work in the kitchens of their own restaurants. They're generally young, talk seriously about food, and believe they are working at an art form. Others are the resident geniuses at wineries, and at hotels where they take the word "guest" seriously. Some of these food people are on farms, working in rich California soil to bring unique produce from the earth. Still others till the waters, and are called aquaculturists. Plush West Coast restaurants also house their share of master chefs who understand that elegance must be redefined from time to time, and who apply French techniques to California products.

Only a few of these creators of California cuisine are California born. Most come from other states, other countries. But when asked as to their allegiance, they're quick to reply, "I'm a Californian."

These are the new tastemakers, the new stylists for California, and for you, and me, and the rest of the country as well.

Those 2 Entertaining Californians

Sophie Porter

Californians are proud of their homes, of the way they live, of their special West Coast style. They're concerned about image, and the way they see themselves is just as important as the way other people see them. Homes are redone often, and new interests are reflected in architecture, landscape, and entertaining. Californians blend aspects of their lives. Business, entertaining, and leisure activities overlap; an important contract may be signed during brunch after tennis at someone's home.

Most entertaining is done at home, and manufacturers of appliances, kitchen gadgets, and tabletop ware say that Californians are their best customers. Crock pots, food processors, convection ovens are known and popular around the country now, but they gained their first big impetus on the West Coast. And having purchased the latest appliance, the most interesting wine rack, and a set of elegant maroon and black lacquerware from the Orient, the next thing to do is show them off—by using them at a brunch, party, or dinner.

Entertaining in California is very much a visual art. How things look is meaningful, and this doesn't mean a platter garnished with parsley or serrated lemon slices. *The look* means the setting—the site for entertaining—and because of the kindness of the climate, Californians use the land, the water, the sky, and the weather the way a clever director would use a set. Californians look outward, and entertaining at home means more than using the dining room, living room, or family room. There's the outdoors, and Californians use it lavishly, serving brunch beside a pool, hot tub, or tennis court. A buffet may be presented in a gazebo, on a terraced lawn overlooking a recently acquired horse farm, or in a newly planted vineyard. Parties may be given on boats—square-hulled houseboats, cabin cruisers, sailboats, and, if money is no object, yachts.

For dinner parties for six, eight, or ten, Californians move indoors. Dinners can be informal gatherings in a newly redone kitchen, complete with Mexican tiled floors and walls, or they can take place in a dining room that looks out over a Japanese garden, complete with stream, bridge, and stone lanterns.

When foreigners come to the United States they are astonished and pleased at the way Americans invite visitors into their homes. In other parts of the world, home is a private place, and casual acquaintances are entertained in restaurants or clubs. If foreigners are enchanted by the openness of Americans, Americans who visit California are equally impressed by the warmth and hospitality extended to them. Californians like to entertain, and they do so with style and ease.

Come for Brunch

Brunch is dear to the hearts of Californians. It fits in with West Coast life style: casual, easy, and often out-of-doors. Brunch may be served beside a pool, tennis court, or hot tub. Swim a few laps, play a set or two, solve the world's problems while lolling in a redwood hot tub. Food acquires extra flavor after activity. What do Californians serve for brunch? It's rarely anything as familiar as Eggs Benedict or a Quiche.

Let's Play Tennis First . . .

Chilled orange juice over ice, garnished with fresh, crushed raspberries
Pita Pocket Sandwiches, filled with Hummus Bi Tahini, Goat Cheese, Lettuce, Cucumbers, and Red Peppers
Christopher Norris's Sunflower Tuna Muffins
Fresh fruit bowl

After the Hot Tub . . .

Chenin Blanc white wine and soda over ice
Tomato-Olive Sorbet
The Brown Derby's Cobb Salad
Sourdough bread
Fruit and Amaretto liqueur

Don't You Love a Barbeque . . .

Zinfandel wine
Smoked salmon trout with crème fraîche
Korean Beef Barbecue
Tossed salad: lettuce, orange segments, and bean sprouts with vinaigrette dressing
Cantaloupe Sorbet

Last Month in Cancun . . .

Margaritas
Sangria
Guacamole served with tortilla chips
Jeff's Carne Asado Burrito Brunch
Salsa Mexicana
Mexican-Style Dessert Coffee

Quick California Takes

Sangria

To prepare Sangria, combine the following ingredients in a two-quart pitcher:

1 bottle Gamay Beaujolais wine
Juice of 3 lemons
Juice of 4 oranges
Peel of 1 lemon
Peel of 1 orange
1 peach, sliced
12 ounces mineral water or club soda
(Californians use Calistoga, their own mineral water)

Stir, and add sugar to taste, if you wish.

We're Giving a Party

A party in California, unless it's a small dinner party, means lots of guests and food served buffet style. The party may be limited to drinks and appetizers, or it may be a full-fledged supper that begins as the sun is setting over the Pacific, and goes on through most of the night. Party food can be trays of sushi and sashimi prepared by a Japanese chef, or it may be a wine and dessert party, just one course, but that course presented in splendid array.

Come By for a Drink Around 7 . . .

White Wine:
Sauvignon Blanc
Gewürztraminer
Red Wine: Gamay, chilled
Caviar Stuffed New Potatoes à la Jim Nassikas
Scot's Cheesecake Hors d'Oeuvre
Kiwi Fruit with Prosciutto Ham
Dilly Avocado Lemon Dip

See You Saturday Night at the Beach . . .

White Wine Kir
Chilled red Gamay Beaujolais
Mineral water on the rocks with a wedge of lime
Rumaki with Figs
Hot Pepper Jelly over Cream Cheese
Tapenade over Fettucine Noodles
Shrimp Curry Pacifica
Oranges in Red Wine

It's Just Wine and Dessert . . .

Wines:
Grenache Rosé
Johannisberg Riesling
Emerald Riesling

Peach Clafouti
Sugared Grape Clusters
Cold Lemon Mousse in the Style of Fournou's Ovens
Chocolate Decadence
Almond Tart

Remember, It's Dinner at Eight . . .

The small seated dinner is the exception to the California rule of many people serving themselves from a lavish buffet. These are the important dinners given for four to ten people, where candles glow, wine and jewels gleam, and the choice of food and wine reflects an added touch of formality.

Champagne
Seeded Camembert Cheese Crisps
Chardonnay wine
Oysters in Saffron Cream Sauce
Cabernet Sauvignon wine
Sonoma County Spice-Cured Rack of Lamb
Sliced Tomato Salad
Baked Praline Ice Cream Pie with Rum Sauce
After-Dinner Hollywood Fig Candies
Espresso

To Begin With: Inventive Appetizers 3

Sophie Porter

The aesthetic principle of "less is more" does not apply in California. Most residents of the golden state know full well that more is definitely more, and that more is also better. That idea is evident in the appetizers served on the West Coast; it's rarely anything as pristine as cheese and crackers. The first course starts the meal with proper panache, and appetizers are often served in such array that they are a meal in themselves.

Caviar Stuffed New Potatoes à la James Nassikas

James Nassikas, owner and inventor of the Stanford Court Hotel in San Francisco, pleases his guests with new food ideas using the latest California products. The following recipe is one enjoyable result of Jim's efforts; it may be prepared with Golden Caviar, the natural, golden-hued whitefish roe, or with any other caviar that is available or affordable.

12 very small red new potatoes
Vegetable oil for deep frying
½ cup sour cream, approximately
8–12 tablespoons Golden Caviar (or any caviar available)

Wash and dry potatoes and place in a shallow baking pan. Bake in a preheated 450° oven for 30 to 35 minutes, or until tender.

Remove the potatoes. Slice in half.

Scoop out the center pulp with a melon-ball cutter or small spoon; reserve both pulp and skins. Mash the pulp slightly and keep warm.

Heat the oil in a small saucepan for deep frying. Drop the potato shells a few at a time into the oil and cook quickly until golden brown and crisp. Drain thoroughly.

Fill each potato shell with a thin layer of mashed potatoes. (It is not necessary to use all the mashed potatoes; it really depends on how much caviar you can afford.) Add a thin layer of sour cream. Top with caviar.

Yield: 24 pieces (serves 6, approximately)

Beringer Vineyards: Developing a Regional California Cuisine

In April, 1981, the Beringer Vineyards of Napa Valley decided to encourage the development of a regional cuisine that would complement the wines of California.

Richard Maher, president of Beringer, contacted Ron Batori, the Dean of the California Culinary Academy in San Francisco, and offered a scholarship to a senior student who would create dishes that best exemplified imaginative, California cooking.

In addition to the scholarship, the winner was also to be granted an eight-week research internship at the winery, where California cooking in general, and Napa Valley cuisine in particular, would be further developed.

Ron Batori, who sees the development of California cuisine going hand-in-hand with the growth of California wines, understood what the Beringer Vineyards wanted.

"A mutual admiration society between food and wine is developing in California," Dean Batori explained, "even the smaller wineries, Trefethen, Rutherford Hill, Joseph Phelps; they're all building test kitchens to develop a cuisine that will complement their wines. And it makes sense. The Burgundy region in France has the rich, hearty cuisine that goes along with their rich Burgundy wines. In the past five years the wine industry here has understood the need for food that would complement their wines."

According to Dean Batori, California cuisine has a definite philosophy, "California cuisine is cuisine bourgeois reinterpreted. We have our own way of preparing bouillabaisse, of preparing dishes with lamb, squab, fish, and fruit. And don't forget, we get fresh produce twelve months of the year. That's bound to make a difference in the way Californians cook.

"At least half of the student body at the California Culinary Academy have bachelor degrees," said Batori, "and most of the students see food as a creative medium."

Fitting the profile of the Academy student, the winner of the Beringer competition was 27-year-old Scot Horrobin, who holds a Bachelor's Degree in biology from San Jose State College. Before becoming a student at the Academy, Scot had no professional cooking experience, and he was another example of a young Californian who decided to become a chef because he thought of food as a creative medium.

The recipes created by Scot to win the competition were: Oysters in Saffron Cream Sauce, Cheese-Stuffed Squab, Bouillabaisse, and Almond

Tart. Since that time, while working at the Beringer kitchens, Scot Horrobin has done increasingly innovative work, developing a special way of preparing rack of lamb, and inventing the following cheesecake that is meant to be served as an appetizer, or in place of a cheese course.

Scot's Cheesecake Hors d'Oeuvre

1½ cups fresh bread crumbs
½ cup sesame seeds
¼ pound butter, melted
1 pound California or French goat cheese
1 pound California cream cheese without additives (or other cream cheese)
6 eggs
½ teaspoon freshly ground white pepper
2 tablespoons finely chopped fresh rosemary

Combine crumbs, sesame seeds, and butter. Mix until thoroughly blended. Press crumb mixture into a 9-inch pie plate or tart pan. Refrigerate for 30 minutes.

Combine all other ingredients and mix until thoroughly blended. A food processor may be used. Spoon cheese mixture into crust.

Bake cheesecake in a preheated 350° oven for about 25 minutes. Crust should not brown and filling should be just barely set, as it will set as it cools.

Serves: 6–8

Rumaki with Figs

A California improvisation: dried figs combined with bacon and water chestnuts—an American invention with Oriental overtones.

12 dried figs (Calimyrna or Mission figs)
24 water chestnuts (8-ounce can)
12 slices bacon, cut in half lengthwise
½ cup soy sauce
¼ cup sherry wine
1 tablespoon sugar
1 clove garlic, pressed
½ teaspoon ground ginger

Snip and discard stems from figs. Cut figs in half. Press water chestnut onto each fig half. Wrap each fig half in a piece of bacon. Secure with toothpick and place in a shallow dish.

Combine soy sauce, sherry, wine, sugar, garlic, and ginger. Mix thoroughly. Pour marinade over figs. Marinate for 2 hours, turning once or twice. Drain. Place figs in a preheated broiler and broil about 8 to 10 minutes, or until bacon is crisp, turning to brown all sides.

Yield: 24

Spicy Olive-Stuffed Won Ton

½ cup minced celery
¼ cup minced green onion or scallions
1 tablespoon vegetable oil
1 tablespoon cornstarch
2 cups pitted ripe olives (black California olives), chopped fine
1 can (6 ounces) water chestnuts, drained, rinsed, and chopped
1 teaspoon ground ginger
1 teaspoon soy sauce
1 teaspoon hot pepper sauce
1 package (12 ounces) won ton skins*
Vegetable oil for deep frying

Sauté celery and onion in 1 tablespoon oil until vegetables are limp. Add cornstarch and stir. Remove from heat.

Add olives, water chestnuts, ginger, and soy sauce. Stir until ingredients are well blended.

To shape won ton, place 1 teaspoon vegetable mixture in center of won ton skin. Moisten edges of skin with water and bring opposite corners together to form a triangle. Press edges to seal. Moisten one corner of fold and press onto other corner. Repeat until all won ton skins are filled.

Deep fry in oil for about 3 minutes, or until won ton is golden brown. Drain on paper towels. Serve with plum sauce.

Yield: 50 won ton, approximately

---

*Won ton skins can be found in the refrigerated or freezer section of most markets, or in groceries specializing in Oriental foods.

Sushi—California Style

One of the biggest food fads on the West Coast is sushi, the Japanese raw fish roll that is traditionally wrapped around a core of pickled rice, then bound together with strips of seaweed. Los Angeles and Hollywood abound in small stands and restaurants advertising "Take-Out Sushi," and Hollywood parties feature chefs who prepare sushi while the guests ooh and aah and debate the merits of salmon versus yellow tail sushi.

Want to give an intimate sushi party for two? Call a sushi caterer and he'll send a chef or a tray of already-prepared sushi just right for a friendly candlelit supper. According to Angelenos, the most elegant sushi party is given on a yacht with a sushi chef ensconced on the after-deck while guests mill about drinking California champagne.

With true hometown spirit, Yamashiro's, a Japanese restaurant high in the Hollywood hills, has developed a very special version of sushi called the California Roll. At one time Yamashiro's was a private home built as an exact replica of a mountain palace in Japan. In 1960 it became a restaurant, and today guests may dine on heated terraces with breathtaking views of Hollywood, Los Angeles, and the Pacific Ocean beyond.

Yamashiro's offers tempura and teriyaki, but, California fashion, it is more eclectic than Oriental; for lunch it's possible to order a Yamashiro Burger—a hamburger topped with spinach, mushrooms, Monterey Jack cheese, served with steak-fried potatoes and fresh fruit. In the evening those who aren't in the mood for the restaurant's special Japanese Feast can always order Veal Oscar—made with crab, asparagus, and Bearnaise sauce.

But with all that, Yamashiro's is justly proud of its Japanese dishes, and has two chefs, Takeru and Masa, who devote all their time to preparing jewel-like sushi rolls, including the very special California Roll.

The following recipes are different as well as delicious, and a great way of introducing sushi to those who are afraid of eating raw fish.

California Sushi Roll

½ cup vinegar
½ cup sugar
1 cup warm cooked rice
2 tablespoons sesame seeds
½ cup cooked crabmeat
3 tablespoons fish roe (may be Golden Caviar)
½ avocado, chopped
Wasabi paste

To prepare rice for this or any other sushi dish rice must be pickled. Combine vinegar and sugar in an enamel saucepan and bring to a boil. Cook, stirring, until sugar is completely dissolved. Remove from heat.

Stir 2 tablespoons of vinegar-sugar mixture into the cooked, still warm, rice. Warm rice absorbs the vinegar-sugar mixture more completely. Stir sesame seeds into rice.

Press pickled rice into a square on a small serving platter. Cut rice into squares, and leave rice squares in place. Press each square lightly so that rice clings, and place a small dab of Wasabi paste on each.

Press a bit of crabmeat, fish roe, and avocado on each square.

At Yamashiro's the chefs fold a bit of crabmeat around the fish roe and top with the avocado. A dab of Wasabi paste is added, and this crabmeat combination is used as a filling for a roll of pickled rice. It's beautiful to look at and delicious to eat; however, if you haven't spent years learning how to prepare sushi, you'll find this an easier method.

Serves: 4

Tamago Sushi in the Style of Yamashiro

2 eggs, lightly beaten
2 tablespoons sake wine (or dry white wine)
1 teaspoon sugar
¼ teaspoon salt
1 tablespoon soy sauce
Vegetable oil
1 cup pickled rice (see California Sushi Roll, above)
Seaweed strips (optional)

Combine eggs, wine, sugar, salt, and soy sauce. Beat until all ingredients are thoroughly mixed.

In a small skillet, omelet or crepe pan, heat a small amount of oil. When oil is hot, make 2 or 3 thin omelets from egg mixture. Place omelets on a damp cloth while still warm.

Divide rice and place a portion down the center of each omelet. Roll jelly-roll fashion and allow to rest, seam side down, for 2 minutes.

Slice filled omelets crosswise to serve, and bind with seaweed strips, if desired.

Serves: 2–3

Olive Pâté

1½ cups drained pitted ripe olives (black California olives)
1 cup grated Monterey Jack cheese
2 hard-cooked eggs, shelled
2 teaspoons brandy
1½ teaspoons dried basil
¾ teaspoon dried tarragon
¼ teaspoon freshly ground black pepper
1 small clove garlic
2 tablespoons minced parsley

Combine olives, cheese, eggs, brandy, basil, tarragon, pepper, and garlic in a food processor or electric blender. Purée until nearly smooth. Spoon into a crock or jar. Cover and chill until ready to serve. Sprinkle with minced parsley and serve with raw vegetables, sliced sourdough bread, or crackers.

Yield: 2½ cups, approximately

Oysters in Saffron Cream Sauce

12 fresh oysters, in the shell, thoroughly scrubbed
½ bottle of California dry Champagne
2 cups heavy sweet cream (whipping cream)
¼ cup demi-glace (homemade or bought in a gourmet food shop)
Pinch of saffron
Salt and freshly ground white pepper to taste
3 tablespoons unsalted butter, softened
2 tablespoons freshly grated Parmesan cheese

Shuck oysters and reserve shells. Combine oyster juices with champagne in a saucepan, and bring to a simmer.

Add oysters and poach until oysters are firm, about 3 minutes. Remove oysters and reserve. Reduce champagne-oyster sauce by one-fourth, and reserve.

Heat cream, and reduce by one-half. Add demi-glace and saffron to cream, and mix until thoroughly combined. Add champagne sauce to cream sauce gradually, stirring. Add seasoning. Remove from heat, and add butter bit by bit, stirring, until butter is incorporated into sauce.

Place 12 oyster shell halves in a shallow baking dish that can be brought to the table. Heat in a preheated 300° oven for 1 or 2 minutes. Shells should be barely warm.

Remove baking dish from oven and place a poached oyster on each shell half. Top with sauce and Parmesan cheese. Place in a preheated broiler for 2 minutes.

Serves: 2–3

Alice Waters and Chez Panisse

Perhaps the most influential chef in California, and maybe in the entire United States, is Alice Waters. Chef Waters had been a student of French cultural history at Berkeley, and went to France to continue her studies. It was there that she discovered what food and good cooking could really be, and when she came back to the United States she decided to open a restaurant in Berkeley.

Alice Waters seems to have been the first to embark on what is now known as California cuisine, combining three elements: expertise in cooking techniques, the best ingredients from California's fields, farms, and waters, and a truly creative and innovative attitude towards cooking.

Chez Panisse opened in the early seventies, and the name of the restaurant came from the Marcel Pagnol film trilogy, "Marius," "Fanny," and "César." In the novels it is César who owns the café in Marseille where all his friends meet, but Alice and her friends discovered that it was too difficult to answer the restaurant phone with a quickly repeated "Chez César," and so the restaurant was named after another important character in the trilogy, Panisse.

Today, Chez Panisse has two dining rooms; the one downstairs is ever-so slightly more formal, with reservations a must, and complete price-fixed dinners, while the room upstairs, Café Chez Panisse, has a casual atmosphere and a menu that includes croustades of bread baked with olive oil, mozarella cheese and olive tapenade served with a lentil salad, chevre cheese marinated in oil and basil, baked and served with salad. Greens for the restaurant's salads sometimes come from Alice Waters's own garden, and it is here you can find the best calzone served on the entire North American continent.

Among the dishes served in the downstairs dining room are a squash tart in a puff-pastry shell, baked quail with a wine, grape juice, and leek sauce, a chevre cheese soufflé, and fresh peach, plum, and pear sorbets. It is no wonder that regular Chez Panisse clients give Alice Waters fifty-two stamped, self-addressed envelopes annually so that they can receive each week's menus and decide on which day they will dine at her restaurant.

Alice Waters has influenced the way people eat and the way people cook. Many young chefs who worked with her at Chez Panisse have gone on to spread the gospel about fresh food and fine cooking: Jeremiah Tower is opening his own restaurant in San Francisco after a stint there at the Balboa Cafe, Deborah Madison is chef at Green's, also in San Francisco, and others have gone on to more elaborate restaurants in Los Angeles and points east.

Herb Toasted Sourdough Bread and Roast Peppers

For a great appetizer, combine thick slices of sourdough bread, toasted and sprinkled with herbs, with roast peppers. Versions of this dish are served at two of San Francisco's most popular restaurants, Green's and Café Chez Panisse.

12 slices sourdough bread (or French bread, or wholewheat Italian bread), 2–3 inches thick
1–2 teaspoons dried rosemary, crushed
½ cup olive oil
Salt and freshly ground black pepper to taste
6 large, sweet, red peppers
6 tablespoons olive oil
2 cloves garlic, pressed (or 1 clove Elephant Garlic, sliced thin)

Place bread slices in preheated broiler and toast until golden brown.

Remove bread from broiler and sprinkle with rosemary. Spoon the ½ cup of olive oil over bread slices, and season with salt and pepper.

Pile bread slices into a deep, napkin-lined plate, and draw ends of napkin over bread to keep it warm.

Pierce peppers with a large fork, and hold over heat until skin chars.

After peppers have cooled somewhat, scrape off charred skin with a knife. Slice peppers, discarding seeds.

Toss the pepper slices with the remaining olive oil and garlic, and serve with the toasted bread.

Serves: 6

Tapenade

Tapenade is traditionally served as a spread for crusty, buttered chunks of French bread. In California, however, tapenade is also used as a sauce for fettucine, or as a filling for 6-inch crêpes served as appetizers.

1 can (2 ounces) rolled fillets of anchovies
2 cups pitted small ripe olives (black California olives)
¼ cup olive oil
Juice of ½ lemon

Combine all ingredients in a food processor or blender, or use mortar and pestle and thoroughly purée all ingredients.

Serve over ½ pound cooked fettucine or wholewheat pasta, or as a filling for 6-8 crêpes.

Yield: 2 cups, approximately

Van Nuys-Style Appetizer

1 pound white fish (Pacific snapper, sea bass, or sole)
Grated peel of 1 lemon
Juice of 3 lemons
2 large tomatoes, chopped
1 cup green chili salsa, homemade or canned
⅓ cup sliced green onions or scallions
3 tablespoons chopped fresh coriander (cilantro), parsley, or celery
     leaves
2 tablespoons vegetable oil
½ teaspoon dried oregano, crushed
¼ teaspoon salt

Cut fish into ½-inch cubes. Combine fish, lemon peel, and juice and cover. Refrigerate for 8 hours or overnight, until fish is opaque and has a "cooked" look. Stir occasionally.

Add remaining ingredients to fish and chill for 30 minutes.

Serves: 6

Kiwi Fruit with Prosciutto Ham

Prosciutto has traditionally been served with melon or fresh figs, but for something really different try thin slices of prosciutto with kiwi fruit.

½ pound prosciutto ham, sliced thin
6 kiwi fruit

Peel kiwi fruit and slice into rounds, approximately ¼-inch thick.
Place prosciutto slices on a serving platter, and surround or top with sliced kiwi fruit.

Serves: 4

Dilled Shrimp in Sour Cream

1½ cups sour cream
4 teaspoons horseradish
¼ cup mayonnaise
2 tablespoons chopped fresh dill
Cognac to taste
½ pound cooked, cleaned small shrimp

Combine all ingredients except shrimp and cognac. Mix thoroughly.
Add 1 or 2 dashes of cognac to shrimp and toss. Combine shrimp and sour cream-horseradish mixture. Toss gently.

Serves: 3–4

Stuffed Mushrooms Delegeane

36 large, fresh mushrooms
¾ cup butter, melted
1 cup chopped fresh dill
4 cloves Elephant Garlic, sliced
¼ medium-size onion
4 teaspoons white wine
2 teaspoons freshly squeezed lemon juice
Salt and freshly ground white pepper to taste

Separate mushroom caps from stems. Set mushroom caps in a shallow, lightly greased baking dish.

Place stems and all other ingredients in a food processor or blender, and purée. Spoon into mushroom caps.

Bake in a preheated 375° oven for 10 minutes, or until sauce begins to bubble.

Place stuffed mushrooms under broiler until tops are golden brown.

Serves: 10–12

Hot Pepper Jelly

It probably started in Texas, but now, hot pepper jelly spooned over a large chunk of cream cheese and served with crackers is a favorite at cocktail time in California. How hot can hot pepper jelly get? It depends on the kind and amount of chili peppers you use. The jelly will be even hotter if you use the tiny seeds within the peppers. Therefore, it may be best to seed the chili peppers the first time around.

Hot chili peppers are red, green, or yellow and they can be bought fresh in many stores around the country, but you may substitute the canned hot chili peppers readily available in most supermarkets that carry ingredients for Mexican-style cookery.

½ cup finely chopped hot chili peppers, seeded or not
2 cups finely chopped green bell peppers, seeded
4 cups sugar
1 cup white vinegar
1 bottle (6 ounces) pectin

Combine all ingredients, except pectin, in a saucepan. Bring to a boil, and cook, stirring constantly, for 5 minutes. Allow to cool for 5 minutes. Add pectin and stir to combine thoroughly. Spoon into jars and refrigerate until jelled.

To serve, place an 8-ounce block of cream cheese on a serving plate. Spoon jelly over cheese, and surround with crackers or tortilla chips.

Yield: 4 cups, approximately

Lemon-Marinated Mushrooms

In addition to the regular mushrooms found in most supermarkets a variety of Oriental mushrooms can now be found in many fruit and vegetable stores. These tiny, white enoki mushrooms are cooked quickly, marinated, and served as a popular appetizer on the West Coast. If the enoki mushrooms are not available, use regular mushrooms.

8 tablespoons olive oil
2 tablespoons red wine vinegar
⅛ teaspoon red pepper flakes
1 clove garlic, pressed
2 pounds mushrooms
1 teaspoon grated lemon peel
2 tablespoons freshly squeezed lemon juice

Combine oil, vinegar, pepper flakes, and garlic in a saucepan. If you're using enoki mushrooms, leave them whole; if you're using regular mushrooms, separate mushroom caps from stems. Add mushrooms to saucepan, and cook for 2 minutes, uncovered, stirring.

Remove from heat and add lemon peel and juice. Refrigerate until chilled. Drain and serve.

Serves: 4–6

Clever Californian Cheese Tricks

For a truly different appetizer or salad course, do as the Californians do; serve a hot cheese dish.

L'Escoffier, the elegant restaurant atop the Beverly Hilton Hotel in Beverly Hills, serves Fried Camembert with a salad of Kentucky lime-stone lettuce, topped with crushed walnuts and a dressing made of walnut oil and lemon juice.

Chez Panisse, Alice Waters's acclaimed Berkeley restaurant, offers Baked Sonoma goat cheese with Garden Lettuces on the menu in the Café Chez Panisse.

Green's at Fort Mason, San Francisco's vegetarian restaurant operated by the Zen Mountain Center, presents a popular Toasted Goat Cheese with Sun-Dried Tomatoes as an appetizer. It seems there's more to life than a grilled cheese sandwich, or even a cheese fondue.

Fried Camembert

8 ounces Camembert cheese (or Brie)
4 tablespoons all-purpose flour
1 or 2 eggs, well beaten
1 cup bread crumbs
4–8 tablespoons butter

This dish can be made with 8 wedges of cheese, or with an 8-ounce round of Camembert which can be cooked in one piece, and then cut like a pie.

Scrape cheese gently. It is not necessary to remove the entire crust; whatever scrapes off with the side of a knife blade is sufficient.

Roll cheese in flour, shaking off any excess. Dip cheese into beaten eggs, and then roll in bread crumbs.

Heat butter in a skillet until hot, and fry cheese. Do not overcook. When crumbs brown on one side, turn cheese quickly to brown on the other. It is important to move quickly, or cheese will melt and seep through coating.

Drain cheese and serve at once, with your favorite salad if you wish.

Serves: 8

Alice Waters's Baked Goat Cheese

8 1-inch rounds of mild fresh goat cheese
1 cup olive oil
1 clove garlic, minced
Freshly ground black pepper to taste
8–12 fresh basil leaves, torn in half
1 cup bread crumbs

Place the cheese in a shallow dish and pour olive oil over it. Turn cheese to coat with oil on all sides.

Sprinkle cheese with garlic and pepper, and toss basil leaves over and around cheese. Let sit in oil for at least 1 hour, basting with oil from time to time.

Before baking, remove cheese rounds from oil, reserving oil, and coat cheese with bread crumbs. Place breaded cheese rounds on a baking dish and bake in a preheated 450° oven for 10 minutes.

Prepare a salad dressing, using reserved oil, and serve cheese with a mixed green salad. Endive and watercress combine very well with baked goat cheese, as do arugula and red leaf lettuce.

Serves: 8

Quick California Takes

Look for *Sun-Dried Tomatoes* packed in olive oil in little glass jars.
Spoon *Sun-Dried Tomatoes* over cold pasta salad, or over a wedge of goat cheese that's been grilled on a thick slice of Italian or French bread.

Seeded Camembert Cheese Crisps

The cheese industry in California is developing its own version of some French favorites. If Camembert comes from California can it be called Camembert? Well, it's called California Camembert, and it's delicious. The following recipe can be made with either the domestic or imported variety. It's best served hot with your favorite chilled champagne (and if you haven't already done so, try a bit of the California bubbly).

8 ounces ripe Camembert cheese
4 tablespoons unsalted butter
1 cup all-purpose flour
⅛ teaspoon cayenne pepper
½ teaspoon salt
Sesame or poppy seeds
Paprika (optional)

Allow butter and cheese to reach room temperature. Place all ingredients except seeds and paprika in a food processor. Using the metal blade, process until mixture forms a ball.
Remove dough from bowl and divide into 2 equal portions. On a sheet of waxed paper, form each portion into a roll 1 to 1½ inches in diameter. Roll in sesame or poppy seeds to cover sides. Sprinkle with paprika, if desired.
Wrap rolls well and refrigerate overnight. (They may be frozen and used at a later date.)

Just before serving, remove from refrigerator (frozen rolls should be thawed but firm) and slice into ¼-inch slices. Place on an ungreased baking sheet and bake in a preheated 400° oven for 10 to 12 minutes. Serve hot.

Yield: 50–60

Cheese Canapes from Buttercup Manor

1 cup grated Monterey Jack cheese
½ cup grated Romano cheese
½ cup grated Parmesan cheese
2 cloves Elephant Garlic, minced
⅓ cup chopped green onions or scallions
½ cup mayonnaise
⅛ teaspoon Dijon mustard
½ cup chopped parsley
Small slices black or rye bread

Combine ingredients in order shown above. Mix thoroughly.

To serve, spread mixture generously on bread slices and place in a preheated broiler until cheese bubbles and is slightly brown.

Yield: 3 cups, approximately

Nutty Cheese Spread

1 cup walnuts
1 cup finely chopped onion
¼ cup butter
1 pound finely chopped fresh mushrooms
¼ cup dry white wine
2 packages (3 ounces each) cream cheese, softened
3 tablespoons chopped parsley
2 tablespoons anchovy paste
2 tablespoons finely chopped pimiento

Spread the walnuts in a baking pan and toast in a preheated 300° oven, stirring once, for about 10 minutes, or until very lightly browned. Remove from oven and cool, then chop fine.

Sauté onion in butter until soft, but not brown. Add mushrooms and sauté for 5 minutes, stirring frequently. Add wine and stir over low heat until liquid is slightly reduced. Cool.

Combine cream cheese, parsley, anchovy paste, and pimiento. Add cooled mushroom mixture, then walnuts. Serve with crackers or cocktail rye bread.

Yield: 3½ cups, approximately

Quick California Takes

Pita Pocket Sandwiches

Split small, individual pita breads and spread with a layer of *hummus bi tahini*. Top with lettuce, cucumbers, slices of sweet red pepper, small cubes of goat cheese, and chopped scallions.

Or combine cottage cheese and blue cheese, mash with a mild fruit vinegar, and spread on split individual pita breads. Top with sliced tomato, diced avocado, sunflower seeds, and bean sprouts.

Hummus Bi Tahini

Combine 2 cups cooked chick peas with 1 tablespoon olive oil, juice of 2 lemons, 2 cloves garlic, ½ cup tahini (sesame seed paste), and ½ cup water in a food processor, and purée. If mixture is too thick, add more water.

Baked Walnut Puffs

½ cup walnuts, lightly toasted
½ cup butter, softened
½ teaspoon ground cumin
½ teaspoon Dijon mustard
½ teaspoon salt
1 teaspoon grated onion
2 cups grated Cheddar cheese
1¼ cups sifted all-purpose flour

Chop walnuts fine. Mix butter, cumin, mustard, salt, onion, and cheese until smooth and well blended. Stir in walnuts and flour. Mix until dough is stiff.

Roll level tablespoons of the dough into small balls and place them on an ungreased cookie sheet.

Bake in a preheated 350° oven for 10 to 15 minutes, or until very lightly browned.

Remove to wire racks. Serve warm or cold.

Yield: 24 to 30

San Francisco Shrimp and Melon Appetizer with Sunset Dressing

2 cantaloupes, peeled, seeded, and sliced into 4 rings each
1½ pounds small shrimp, cooked, shelled, and deveined

Place each cantaloupe ring on a plate. Divide the shrimp into 8 portions and pack each portion into an ice cream scoop, then gently squeeze to extract a little liquid. Place a mound of shrimp on top of each melon ring.

Sunset Dressing

1½ cups mayonnaise
½ cup catsup
½ cup red wine vinegar
⅓ cup finely chopped sweet pickles
Salt to taste
Dash of freshly ground black pepper
4 tablespoons toasted shredded coconut

Combine mayonnaise, catsup, vinegar, and chopped pickle in a small bowl. Add salt and pepper and blend. Spoon dressing over each serving.

Sprinkle toasted coconut on top of each portion.

Serves: 8

Dilly Avocado Lemon Dip

1 large avocado, peeled and pitted
1 cup sour cream
1 teaspoon freshly grated lemon peel
2 tablespoons freshly squeezed lemon juice
1 clove garlic, pressed
½ teaspoon chopped fresh dillweed
⅛ teaspoon hot pepper sauce

In a bowl, mash avocado well (or use a food processor), then gradually blend in sour cream. Stir in lemon peel and juice, garlic, dill, and hot pepper sauce; chill. Serve as a dip with assorted fresh vegetables such as cauliflower pieces, carrot and celery sticks, and cherry tomatoes.

Yield: 2 cups, approximately

Eggplant-Olive Appetizer

1 eggplant (about 1 pound)
2 medium-size green peppers
3 tablespoons olive oil
3 tablespoons red wine vinegar or lemon juice
1 large tomato, peeled, seeded, and finely chopped
2 tablespoons finely chopped fresh parsley
1 clove garlic, minced
1 cup pitted ripe olives (black California olives) coarsely chopped
Salt and freshly ground black pepper to taste
2–3 ounces feta cheese

Peel eggplant and slice into ½-inch slices, lengthwise. Sprinkle with salt and let stand in a colander for 20 to 30 minutes. Rinse and pat dry on paper towels. Cut into cubes and steam until soft. Allow to cool.

Roast the peppers by piercing with a fork and turning over a low flame until the skin chars and cracks. Peel and discard the skin and the pepper seeds.

In a blender or food processor, purée the eggplant. Reserve. Chop the peppers fine and combine with eggplant. Stir in oil and vinegar and blend well.

Stir in chopped tomato, parsley, and garlic. Add chopped olives and season with salt and pepper. Top with feta cheese.

Serve with buttered French or pita bread.

Serves: 6–8

Crab St. Jacques

1 package (6–8 ounces) frozen Alaska King crab meat or 1 cup fresh
      crab meat
½ cup sliced fresh mushrooms
2 green onions or scallions, sliced
1 tablespoon butter
2 teaspoons cornstarch
2 tablespoons water
½ cup heavy cream
1 tablespoon dry white wine
1 tablespoon freshly squeezed lemon juice
¼ teaspoon salt
¼ teaspoon dried thyme
⅛ teaspoon white pepper
1 tablespoon bread crumbs
1 tablespoon grated Parmesan cheese
1 tablespoon melted butter

Thaw, drain, and slice crab. Sauté mushrooms and green onions in butter. Add crab and heat through. Blend cornstarch and water and add to crab. Add cream, wine, and lemon juice.

Cook, stirring constantly, until thickened and smooth. Blend in seasonings.

Divide among 2 or 3 scallop shells or individual *au gratin* dishes.

Combine bread crumbs, Parmesan cheese, and melted butter; sprinkle over casseroles. Place in preheated broiler 3 to 5 inches from heat for 3 to 4 minutes, or until lightly browned.

Serves: 2–3

Five O'Clock Fritters

1 cup bread crumbs
1 cup grated Cheddar cheese (about 4 ounces)
3 eggs, beaten
½ cup minced onion
¼ cup minced parsley
½ teaspoon curry powder
¼ teaspoon cardamom
2 cups pitted ripe olives (black California olives) finely chopped
Butter for frying

Combine crumbs, cheese, eggs, onion, parsley, curry powder, and cardamom in a bowl. Mix thoroughly. Add olives and mix again. Divide into 8 portions. Shape each portion into a ball. Heat butter in a skillet and fry the fritters on both sides until well browned.

Serves: 4

For a 4 Different Brunch

Sophie Potter

Brunch, for many Californians, is a weekly rite. It's far more involved than Eggs Benedict served with a Bloody Mary.

Because Californians lead a more outdoor life, brunch is frequently served after tennis or beside the pool, and may consist of course after course of food. Many people prepare brunch dishes that have a Mexican or Oriental flavor, and brunch may go on through most of Sunday. Some brunch favorites are prepared on the barbeque grill, and late in the afternoon dessert is brought out, usually a fruit and ice cream concoction or a light fruit dessert.

Tomato-Olive Sorbet

A perfect first course on a hot summer's day is this refreshing, West Coast version of gazpacho which has been converted from a soup to a sorbet.

1 envelope unflavored gelatin
2 cups tomato juice
1½ tablespoons vinegar
3 drops hot pepper sauce
2 egg whites
¾ cup pitted ripe olives (black California olives) chopped
¼ cup finely chopped, peeled, and seeded cucumber
3 tablespoons finely chopped green pepper
1 teaspoon finely chopped green onion or scallions

Soften gelatin in ½ cup tomato juice. Heat remaining tomato juice and add softened gelatin to hot tomato juice. Stir until gelatin is completely dissolved. Add vinegar and hot pepper sauce. Pour into ice cube tray, and freeze until almost solid.

Approximately 45 minutes to 1 hour before serving, remove tomato mixture from freezer and let stand at room temperature for a few minutes to soften slightly.

Cut mixture into small cubes, and spoon into a deep bowl. Beat with a rotary beater until mixture becomes smooth. Add egg whites, and beat rapidly until mixture is light and fluffy. Stir in olives, cucumber, green pepper, and onion. Sorbet may be served immediately, or returned to freezer for 45 minutes to 1 hour.

Serves: 6

Stacked Ricotta Pancakes with Fruit

1 cup ricotta cheese
3 eggs
¼ cup wholewheat flour
1 tablespoon brown sugar
Butter

In a blender or food processor make pancake batter by combining cheese, eggs, flour, and sugar. Blend until smooth.

Coat large skillet or griddle lightly with butter. Heat over medium heat. Pour batter into skillet, using ¼ cup for each pancake. Turn pancakes over when bubbles form on surface; brown other side.

Place a pancake in a baking dish. Top with a heaping tablespoon of apple sauce, apple-plum butter, or your favorite preserve. Place another pancake on top, and continue alternating pancakes and filling, finishing with fruit.

Place stacked pancakes in a preheated 350° oven for 10 minutes. Serve by cutting stacked pancakes into wedges.

Serves: 4

Buckwheat Crêpes with Caviar

¼ cup butter, melted
1 cup milk
¼ cup buckwheat flour
¾ cup all-purpose flour
Pinch of salt
2 eggs
1 teaspoon vegetable oil
½ cup beer
Butter for cooking crêpes
1 pint sour cream, plain yogurt, or crème fraîche for filling
Golden caviar, or salmon caviar

Combine first 8 ingredients in a food processor or blender. Blend until thoroughly smooth. Allow mixture to rest in refrigerator for at least 1 hour.

Cook crêpes in a non-stick skillet or crêpe pan, using a small amount of butter to coat the pan. Reserve crêpes.

Place a tablespoon of sour cream, yogurt, or crème fraîche on each crêpe, top with approximately 1 teaspoonful of your favorite caviar. Roll each crêpe and place in a shallow, ovenproof baking dish.

To serve, heat filled crêpes in a preheated 350° oven for 5 to 10 minutes.

Serves: 8–10

Buckwheat crêpes may also be used with a sweet filling of preserves, fruit butter, or fruit compote. If using a sweet filling, add 1 teaspoon of sugar to crêpe batter.

Homemade Apricot Preserves for Buckwheat Crêpes

5 cups sliced fresh apricots
3½–4 cups sugar
¼ cup lemon juice

Combine sliced apricots, sugar, and lemon juice.
Cook until thick. Pour into sterilized jars, allowing ½ inch at the top. Seal while hot.

Yield: 2 pints, approximately

Crab and Vegetable Omelet

1 package (6–8 ounces) frozen Alaska King crab meat (or 1 cup
      fresh crab meat)
1 small zucchini
¾ cup sliced fresh mushrooms
¼ cup finely chopped onion
1–1½ tablespoons olive oil
4 eggs
¾ teaspoon salt
⅛ teaspoon pepper
⅛ teaspoon dried basil
Pinch of dried oregano
1 tablespoon chopped fresh parsley
Grated Parmesan cheese

Thaw, drain, and slice crab. Slice zucchini and cut slices in half. Sauté zucchini, mushrooms, and onion in oil in 9-inch skillet. Add crab and heat through. Beat eggs; blend in seasonings. Pour eggs over crab mixture; sprinkle with parsley.

Cook over low heat, lifting edges to allow the uncooked portion to run underneath. When set, sprinkle with cheese and place under hot broiler until top is delicately browned. Cut into wedges and serve at once.

Serves: 2

Thirty-Minute Ham and Fig Brunch for Two

1 pound fully cooked ham steak
2 tablespoons butter
1 cup sliced dried Calimyrna figs
2 tablespoons brown sugar
⅛ teaspoon ground cloves
¼ teaspoon dry mustard
⅓ cup port wine

Heat butter in a skillet and lightly sauté ham on both sides.
Stir in sliced figs, brown sugar, cloves, mustard, and wine.
Cover and simmer for 10 minutes.
Serve with rice and a green salad.

Serves: 2

Quick California Takes

Grapes 'n Granola

Place ½ cup seedless green grapes in cereal bowl. Sprinkle with ¼ cup granola and top with yogurt. A natural and healthy breakfast.

A West Coast Pretty

Place 1 strawberry, grape, or raspberry in each compartment of ice cube tray. Fill with water, freeze, and serve white wine or white grape juice over these fruited ice cubes.

Jeff's Carne Asado Burrito Brunch

1½ pounds boneless sirloin steak
4 tablespoons soy sauce
2 tablespoons Worcestershire sauce
Juice of ½ lemon
2 cloves garlic, pressed
Salt and freshly ground black pepper to taste
6–8 burritos (wheat flour tortillas)
Sour cream
Salsa Mexicana (see p. 134)

Cut steak into thin slices and place in a shallow dish.

Combine soy sauce, Worcestershire sauce, lemon juice, garlic, and seasoning. Mix thoroughly and pour over meat. Allow meat to marinate for 4 hours, turning the slices from time to time.

Remove meat from marinade and cook by barbecuing over a hot charcoal fire, or broiling in a hot oven. Brush a small amount of marinade on meat, and turn once. Cook meat for approximately 5 to 7 minutes.

Heat burritos, and allow guests to serve themselves by placing steak slices on tortillas, and garnishing with sour cream and Salsa Mexicana. Roll burritos and eat out of the hand.

Serves: 4–6

Frontier Flapjacks with Prune Sauce

2 cups pitted prunes
1½ cups water
¼ teaspoon ground ginger
¼ teaspoon ground cardamom
Juice of ½ lemon
5 tablespoons molasses
1½ cups buttermilk
¾ cup rolled oats
1 egg, beaten
½ cup all-purpose flour
½ teaspoon salt
½ teaspoon baking soda
3–4 tablespoons butter

Combine prunes, water, ginger, cardamom, and lemon juice in a large saucepan. Cook over medium heat for approximately 10 minutes, or until prunes are tender. Add 4 tablespoons of the molasses, and cook, stirring, for an additional 3 minutes. Reserve sauce.

Combine buttermilk and oats in a large bowl and mix. Add egg, and mix again. Stir in flour, salt, baking soda, and remaining 1 tablespoon molasses. Mix thoroughly.

Lightly butter a griddle or skillet and place over medium heat. When it is hot, ladle 3 tablespoons of batter on the griddle or skillet for each flapjack. Cook, turning once, until lightly browned on both sides.

Serve flapjacks with prune sauce.

Serves: 4–5

Smoked Brisket of Beef

1 beef brisket (9–11 pounds)
Coarsely ground black pepper
Coarse (kosher) salt to taste
6–8 tablespoons vegetable oil

Season brisket on all surfaces with pepper and salt. Spoon oil over meat, and place in a shallow baking pan in a preheated 350° oven. Roast brisket for 30 minutes per pound.

Prepare a mesquite charcoal or regular charcoal fire. Remove brisket from oven and place on grill over charcoal fire. Cook for 1 hour to smoke meat.

Serves: 12–15, approximately

Quick California Takes

Brunch with Christopher Norris

What does a television actress serve for Sunday brunch? Christopher Norris keeps it simple. The emphasis is on fresh fruit, and the big Hollywood two: avocado and sunflower seeds. Here are three of Christopher's favorites for brunch.

Filled Avocado

Cut an avocado in half. Remove pit. Place 1 or 2 tablespoons jellied consommé madrilene in each avocado half. Top with 1 tablespoon yogurt or sour cream. Add 1 teaspoon of caviar.

Sunflower Tuna Muffin

Split an English muffin. Spread with tuna salad. Top with a slice of pepper cheese. Or top with a slice of Swiss or Muenster cheese and ½ teaspoon chopped, canned, hot jalapeño chili peppers. Sprinkle with chopped sunflower seeds. Grill until cheese has melted slightly.

Fruit and Amaretto

Slice 2 or 3 peaches. Cube ½ casaba melon and add to peaches. Add ½ cup blueberries and 1 cup sliced strawberries. Mix gently. Spoon fruit into parfait glasses, and top with heavy sweet cream. Spoon 1 or 2 tablespoons Amaretto or similar liqueur into each glass. What could be simpler?

Apricot-Vanilla Chantilly

1½ cups puréed fresh apricots
1 tablespoon freshly squeezed lemon juice
¾ cup sugar
1 quart vanilla ice cream
½ cup heavy cream (whipping cream)
¼ teaspoon almond extract

Combine purée, lemon juice, and sugar. Chill for 30 minutes. Soften ice cream slightly. Whip cream and blend in the almond extract. Combine purée, ice cream, and whipped cream quickly but not thoroughly, just enough for a ripple effect. Freeze until firm.

Serves: 6–8

Frozen Peach Dessert

5 medium peaches (about 1½ pounds)
¼ teaspoon almond extract
¾ cup sugar
1 teaspoon freshly squeezed lemon juice
1 cup sour cream

Pit and slice 4 of the peaches. Reserve remaining peach for garnish. Using a food processor or blender, combine peaches with remaining ingredients.

Spoon mixture into a shallow pan or ice cube tray. Freeze until almost firm. Turn into mixer bowl and beat until smooth, but not melted.

Return to freezer or spoon dessert into a mold and freeze again.

To serve, remove from freezer and unmold onto a platter. If you don't wish to use a mold, dessert can be spooned into individual dessert dishes after being frozen the second time.

Pit and slice remaining peach and garnish dessert with slices.

Serves: 4

Baked Figs in Wine

1 pound dried figs
1 cup finely chopped blanched toasted almonds
¼ cup honey
1½ cups muscatel or port wine
½ cup heavy sweet cream (whipping cream), whipped

Cut stems off figs and discard. Separate figs and place in a steamer over ½ inch of boiling water. Cover and steam until figs are well plumped, about 10 minutes. Allow to cool.

Cut each fig on one side, being careful not to cut through, and open gently. Combine almonds and honey and fill each fig. Press to close.

Place figs in a shallow baking dish. Pour wine over figs and place in a preheated 325° oven for 20 to 25 minutes, or until hot. Baste occasionally.

Serve hot, topped with whipped cream.

Serves: 6–8

Quick California Takes

For a Different Breakfast:

Prepare buttered toast. Top with thinly sliced pears. Sprinkle brown sugar over pears, and broil for a minute or so, or until sugar bubbles.

For a Different Lunch:

Take 6 slices of white bread. Spread 3 slices with a combination of peanut butter mixed with a favorite jam—raspberry, perhaps?—and top with remaining bread.

Dip sandwiches in an egg and milk mixture, sauté in hot butter, and you have California Toast instead of ordinary French Toast.

A Sampling 5
of Soups

Sophie Porter

The California soup course emphasizes the fruits and vegetables grown in that state. While an occasional bean soup is served in ranching country, the more popular soups build on a base of chicken stock enhanced with vegetables such as artichokes, lettuce, tomatoes, or carrots. Soups are frequently enriched with heavy cream, because Californians see nothing wrong in combining *natural* with *hedonistic* to create their unique cuisine.

Cream of Artichoke Soup with Crushed Hazelnuts

8 large artichokes
2 tablespoons hazelnuts
6 cups chicken stock or broth
1 cup heavy cream (whipping cream)
Salt and freshly ground white pepper to taste
2 tablespoons sherry wine

Remove all leaves and stems from the artichokes. Clean and scoop out the prickly choke to utilize bottoms only. Cook artichoke bottoms in water approximately 1 hour, or until tender.

Roast hazelnuts in a preheated 250° oven for 10 minutes, or until golden brown. Grind hazelnuts fine.

Combine artichoke bottoms, chicken stock, and hazelnuts in a saucepan. Simmer for 15 minutes.

Pour the mixture into a food processor, blender, or food mill and purée thoroughly. Return soup to saucepan and stir in cream, seasonings, and sherry. Heat gently before serving.

Serves: 8

Easy Cream of Artichoke Soup

1 jar (6 ounces) marinated artichoke hearts
1 clove garlic, pressed
½ cup chopped onion
2 tablespoons all-purpose flour
4 cups chicken broth
1 cup heavy sweet cream (whipping cream)
1 tablespoon finely chopped fresh parsley

Drain marinade from artichoke hearts into a saucepan and reserve the hearts. Add garlic to saucepan. Add onion and cook, covered, for 5 minutes over low heat. Blend in flour. Slowly stir in half the broth, and heat to boiling, stirring constantly. Cook for 1 minute, or until mixture thickens. Place artichoke hearts in food processor or blender. Add hot mixture, and blend until smooth. Pour into saucepan. Add remaining broth and cream. Heat, but do not boil. Sprinkle each serving with parsley.

Serves: 4

Santa Ynez Valley Bean and Chili Soup

1 pound pink, red, or pinto beans
6 to 8 cups boiling water
1 clove garlic, chopped
1 large onion, chopped
¼ teaspoon dried thyme
¼ teaspoon dried marjoram
3 cups beef broth
2 cups stewed tomatoes
1 package (1⅝ ounces) chili seasoning mix or 1 can (7–10 ounces)
    green chili salsa

Sort and wash the beans. Place in a large saucepan and cover with 6 cups water. Bring to a boil. Boil for 3 minutes. Remove from heat, cover, and let stand for 1 hour. Drain beans. Return beans to pot and add boiling water, garlic, onion, thyme, and marjoram to beans.

Cover and simmer until beans are tender, about 2½ to 3 hours. Don't let beans boil dry. Add hot water to cover as needed. Spoon out 3 cups of the cooked beans to use another day in a salad.

Mash rest of beans with their liquid. Add remaining ingredients. Heat 30 minutes.

Serves: 6–8

Cream of Carrot and Tomato Soup

2 tablespoons butter
1 pound carrots, scraped and sliced
1 cup chopped onion
1 clove garlic, minced or pressed
8 medium tomatoes (about 2 pounds), peeled and chopped
2 cups chicken broth
½ teaspoon dried basil
½ teaspoon dried thyme
1 teaspoon salt
⅛ teaspoon freshly ground white pepper
⅛ teaspoon freshly grated nutmeg
1 cup light cream
2 tablespoons chopped fresh parsley

In a large saucepan, melt the butter. Add carrots, onion, and garlic; cook 5 minutes. Reserve ½ cup of the tomatoes and add the rest to the saucepan. Add chicken broth, basil, thyme, salt, pepper, and nutmeg. Bring to a simmer. Cover and simmer for 30 minutes, or until vegetables are tender.

In a food processor, blender, or food mill, purée carrot-tomato mixture thoroughly. Pour into a large bowl and stir in cream. Chill thoroughly. Stir in reserved chopped tomato and sprinkle with parsley before serving.

Serves: 6

Mirassou Winery and Chef Andre Mercier

Because many Californians want to cook the foods that will complement their favorite California wines, the Mirassou Winery in San Jose hired master chef Andre Mercier to conduct a series of cooking classes right at the winery.

Maitre Mercier, who is the owner of Oakland's elegant Mirabeau Restaurant, teaches a variety of cooking techniques, including *nouvelle cuisine*, baking with puff pastry, traditional French cuisine, and preparing the perfect holiday dinner.

Chef Mercier has definite ideas about *nouvelle cuisine*, however, and insists that it is not all that new. "*Nouvelle cuisine* is really a return to the old way of French cooking, the traditional way. It's a form of *haute cuisine* where, for example, sauces are thickened by reduction rather than by the addition of flour. There's nothing really new about that."

How does the concept of French *nouvelle cuisine* combine with the new ideas in California cuisine? The definitions are remarkably similar: *nouvelle cuisine* is based on cooking the best of seasonal ingredients with a light and creative touch, and completing each dish with a delicate sauce and an imaginative garnish. Much of the new California cooking has the same intent, and Mercier's cooking classes are a happy combination of French and California attitudes. Some of the dishes prepared in his classes are Cream of Lettuce Soup, Squab with Garlic Sauce, Cantaloupe Tart, and Barbecued Scallops.

In addition to conducting cooking classes, Andre Mercier and his staff also cater the Sunday Brunches and Sunset Dinners served at the winerys. These events are open to the public and feature delicious combinations of foods and wines served in the winery gardens.

A typical dinner begins with an aperitif of Mirassou au Naturel Champagne served with Camembert Cheese Crisps, a chilled Cream of Lettuce Soup follows with a Riesling, and Artichokes with Bay Shrimp and a lemon sauce are offered with a Monterey Fumé. A Pacific Seafood Terrine comes next, served with a Chardonnay, and a Beaujolais Sorbet is offered to clean the palate.

Afterwards there is a course of Roast Quail served with Zinfandel, an Avocado and Orange Salad with Chenin Blanc, and Strawberries Romanoff with Mirassou's own dessert wine, Fleuri Blanc.

It is no wonder that tickets to these dinners are quickly sold out.

Chef Mercier feels that California inspires good cooking.

"People involved with food, people who love food, are especially progressive in California. They love to try new things. And there are so many new varieties of food—it's incredible.

"There are new types of melon, for example, two kinds of persimmon, and now someone is trying to grow truffles. There's already a crop of Belgian endives growing here, and snails are being raised in California. And have you seen our Golden Caviar? And our California cheese? We've always had Monterey Jack, but now there's some marvelous California Camembert and Chèvre as well."

According to Andre Mercier, "It was the young hippies some years ago who started the whole idea of returning to good foods. Natural foods, wholewheat breads, that sort of thing; that was their idea, they started the trend, and now all of California loves it."

Californians are more health conscious, says Mercier, and want dishes that are both healthful and innovative. There's nothing plain or pipe-rack about most of the food served on the West Coast, and it would be unusual to find a broiled fish fillet or a cooked vegetable without some kind of garnish or sauce.

Cream of Lettuce Soup

1 cup chopped onions
⅓ cup chopped celery
3 tablespoons sweet butter
1 tablespoon all-purpose flour
4 cups chicken stock or broth
1 head Boston (butter) lettuce, washed, trimmed and coarsely
    chopped
1 head escarole, washed, trimmed, and coarsely chopped
1½ teaspoons salt
¼ teaspoon freshly ground white pepper
1 teaspoon dried savory
2 cups light cream

Over medium heat, sauté onions and celery in butter until soft and translucent, about 5 minutes. Add flour and cook, stirring, for 3 minutes. Slowly whisk in the chicken stock and continue stirring until mixture comes to a boil. Stir in both lettuces, salt, pepper, and savory and simmer, stirring occasionally, for 15 minutes. Allow to cool slightly.

Using a food processor, blender, or food mill, purée the soup. Transfer to a bowl and stir in cream. Combine thoroughly and refrigerate until chilled.

Serves: 6–8

Nectarine-Tomato Refresher

2 medium nectarines, diced
½ cup fresh French bread cubes
1½ cups tomato juice
1 medium clove garlic, diced
1 medium tomato, diced
2 tablespoons onion, coarsely chopped
2 tablespoons olive oil
2 teaspoons red wine vinegar
½ teaspoon salt
Pinch of cayenne pepper
1 cup plain yogurt
1 small cucumber, peeled and diced

Combine all ingredients, except for yogurt and cucumber, in a food processor, blender, or food mill. Process until smooth. Chill 4 hours. Garnish with yogurt and diced cucumber.

Serves: 4

Beringer Vineyards Tomato Chicken Soup

10 large ripe tomatoes
1 medium onion, chopped
4 tablespoons butter
2 quarts chicken broth
1 boned and cooked chicken breast, cut into ½-inch cubes
½ cup heavy cream (whipping cream)
8 fresh basil leaves, torn into small pieces
Salt and freshly ground black pepper to taste

Peel, seed, and chop 8 of the tomatoes. In a skillet, sauté chopped tomatoes and onion in 2 tablespoons of the butter until onion is wilted.

Using a food processor, blender, or food mill, purée tomato-onion mixture. Return mixture to skillet, and simmer over low heat, stirring frequently, until tomato-onion mixture is reduced to a paste.

Heat chicken broth and add tomato-onion paste to broth, stirring to combine thoroughly.

Peel, seed, and chop remaining 2 tomatoes, and sauté in 2 tablespoons butter for 5 minutes. Add cubed chicken and cook 5 minutes longer.

Add tomato-chicken mixture to broth and stir to combine.

Off heat, stir in cream. Add basil, salt, and pepper.

Heat gently before serving.

Serves: 10

Turkey Tortilla Soup

3 corn tortillas
2 tablespoons vegetable oil
1 small onion, chopped
2 tablespoons tomato purée
4 cups well-seasoned turkey or chicken stock
¼ cup chopped parsley
1 jalapeño pepper, seeded and chopped fine
1 cup diced cooked turkey
¼ teaspoon freshly squeezed lemon juice
Dash of cayenne pepper
Grated Monterey Jack cheese

Cut tortillas into strips about ¼ inch wide and reserve. Heat oil in large saucepan or Dutch oven. Sauté onion in oil until soft. Stir in tomato purée, stock, parsley, jalapeño pepper, turkey, lemon juice, cayenne, and the tortilla strips. Bring to a simmer and cook for 15 minutes, stirring. Serve with grated cheese.

Serves: 6

A Big Garden Called California: Vegetables and Salads

Sophie Porter

The base of California cuisine is fresh-picked California produce. Everything seems to grow easily and abundantly in California: lettuce, strawberries, citrus fruits, melons, almonds, walnuts, pistachios, tomatoes, garlic, spinach, chanterelle mushrooms, truffles, herbs of all kinds; the list is endless. And every generation of those who cook has its favorites. Some time back rhubarb was popular; today it's avocado. Grapefruit broiled with a bit of brown sugar was once the elegant first course; today it's kiwi fruit with prosciutto.

Some of these fruits and vegetables are favored because they adapt well to a cuisine with an emphasis on nutrition, others because they relate to an ethnic base that has been molded to California life style, and still others because they're new, the latest thing, and marry imaginatively with a variety of foods. It's all done with a let's-try-it spirit, a willingness to experiment, a creative desire for the different, the delicious, and the healthful.

What follows is a brief biography of some of the produce that now appears frequently in California cuisine. Is there a pattern? Most of the fruits and vegetables are low in calories and high in nutrition, and where calories rise it is due to natural fruit sugars, and the appeal of the real and the natural is another California-inspired concept.

Apricots 97% of all apricots grown in the United States come from the orchards in the San Joaquin Valley. Apricots come in three main varieties: Royals, Blenheims, and Tiltons. Apricots were known to exist in China in 2200 B.C., and Biblical scholars say that the apple in the garden of Eden may really have been an apricot. Apricots were brought to Mexico by the Spaniards, and arrived in California via Spanish missionaries in the early 18th century. Apricots are a good source of Vitamins A and C. A fresh apricot contains 18 calories, and ½ cup of dried apricots contains 195 calories.

Artichokes were originally eaten by Arabs, and found their way to Italy in the 15th century. They spread to the rest of Europe, were brought by the French to Louisiana, and by Spanish explorers to California. Today, America's artichokes come from 10,000 or so acres, just south of San Francisco. An artichoke contains 58 calories and is a good source of Vitamins B and C.

Avocado An avocado is a fruit, not a vegetable. Like any plant product, an avocado contains no cholesterol, this despite the avocado's rich, buttery texture and taste. Avocados came to California from Mexico, and depending on which historian you read, they were either the "fruit" or the "butter" of the Aztecs, and are pictured in hieroglyphics found in Aztec ruins. Today, seven California counties produce 80% of all avocados produced in the United States. Avocados are a source of iron, potassium, and Vitamins A, B, C, and E, and contain approximately 132 calories per half avocado, or about 17 calories per slender slice.

Bartlett Pears come mainly from the Sacramento Valley and the lake and mountain districts of northern California. The California Bartlett is a descendant of a wild English pear, which was brought to Massachusetts in the 1790s. The pears flourished on the estate of Enoch Bartlett, and were brought to California during gold rush days. Bartlett pears contain minerals, fiber, B and C Vitamins, and 100 calories each.

Beans California produces eight varieties of colorful beans which are dried and shipped to the rest of the country. Some West Coast favorites are garbanzos or chick peas which are used in Mexican-style cooking, dark or light red kidney beans found in chili, and pink beans which gussy up many a salad. Dry beans are loaded with protein, and are a good source of minerals and the B-complex Vitamins. Depending on the bean, four ounces of cooked dry beans contain from 110 to 120 calories.

Figs ripen fully on the tree, and then semi-dry on the tree as well. They are harvested only after they fall to the ground from their own sweet weight, and are loaded with natural fruit sugars as well as with high nutritional values, including lots of calcium and phosphorus. Figs were brought to California by the Franciscan monks in 1769, and the two most popular types of dried California figs are Calimyrna figs, a mellow, golden brown, and Mission figs, a luscious, purplish black. They are a marvelous natural snack, and three large dried figs equal 200 calories.

Grapes There are 16 major varieties of table grapes grown in California, which means that one or another type of grape is available throughout the year. The names are romance in themselves: Perlette, Almeria, Calmeria, and Lady Fingers, to name a few. Grapes were in North America when the Vikings landed, hence their name of Vinland for the new land. European grapevines were brought to California by the Spanish mission fathers, and California produces 91% of the grapes eaten in the United States. Grapes are low in sodium, they supply fiber, and contain 100 calories per cup.

Kiwi fruit, which came mainly from New Zealand until recently, are now grown in California. The delicate green fruit can be used in desserts, salads, or combined with fish and meat dishes. One kiwi fruit contains only a third of the calories in an orange and twice as much Vitamin C.

Olives The black, mellow beauties known as ripe olives originate in California. The olive is green and bitter when it comes from the tree, but thanks to a curing process created by Freda Ehrmann in the early 1900s, the olive mellows in both flavor and color until it reaches a peak of rich flavor and an even brown-black color. Padre Junipero Serra brought olive cuttings to California in 1769, and today, ripe olives are available around the country year round. Ripe olives are a good source of Vitamin A and calcium and may contain anywhere from 4 to 18 calories per olive, depending on size.

Nectarines are grown mainly in the San Joaquin Valley, and though cousin to the peach, a nectarine is not a cross between a peach and a plum, but rather a fruit that probably developed before the peach, and is related to the rose and almond families as well. The nectarine was a delicacy in ancient China, and botanists today still debate its origin. What is known about this fragrant fruit is that it is a good source of Vitamin C and contains 90 calories. There are 12 types of nectarines grown in California, some freestone, such as the Fantasia and Flavortop, and others clingstone, Flamekist and Late Le Grand, to name two.

Peaches The peach came to California with the first Spanish explorers, and became a California crop in the early part of the 19th century. Peaches from California represent an eighth of the world's supply, and contain Vitamins A and C as well as 40 calories per peach.

Plums there are over 140 varieties of plums grown in the valleys and foothills of California. Some of the more familiar types are the round, red Santa Rosa, the pointy, green Kelsey, the black-red Nubiana, and the deep purple Friar, a new variety growing fast in popularity thanks to its long shelf life. A plum contains only 32 calories, a boon for the weight conscious, and A, B, and C Vitamins.

Prunes are not what happens to leftover plums. There is a special crop of prune plums grown in Northern and Central California, and they're marvelous for natural snacks and for adding a fillip to meats as well as desserts. More prunes are produced in California than in any other part of the world, and this sweet, dry fruit is a source of potassium and Vitamin A. There are 274 calories in 10 extra-large prunes.

Corn and Artichoke Chili Bonanza

6 large artichokes
2 packages (10 ounces each) frozen whole kernel corn, cooked, drained, and cooled
⅔ cup chopped green pepper
¾ cup cooked sliced carrots
2 tablespoons finely chopped onion
1½ cups mayonnaise
3 teaspoons chili powder
¼ teaspoon freshly ground black pepper
2½ teaspoons freshly squeezed lemon juice

Wash artichokes and, using a sharp knife, cut off stalks and about ½ inch of the tops of the artichokes. Trim off tough, outer leaves around the bottoms of each artichoke.

Place artichokes in a saucepan with enough water to almost cover. Cover, and cook for about 1 hour, or until artichokes are tender.

Remove artichokes from saucepan, invert on a board or plate, and drain thoroughly.

When they have cooled, turn artichokes right side up and gently pull open the center leaves. Remove a few of the center leaves, leaving a space to hold the filling. Set artichokes aside.

Combine corn, green pepper, carrots, onion, ½ cup of the mayonnaise, and 2 teaspoons of the chili powder. Mix thoroughly and refrigerate.

Combine remaining cup of mayonnaise, remaining teaspoon of chili powder, seasonings, and lemon juice.

Stuff artichokes with the chilled corn mixture. Top with the seasoned mayonnaise and serve.

Serves: 6

Artichokes 'n Hot Corn

If you prefer your artichokes hot, try the following stuffed artichoke recipe. Cook artichokes according to preceding recipe and prepare them for stuffing as soon as they have cooled enough to handle them.

8 slices bacon, diced
1 cup chopped green pepper
⅓ cup chopped onion
2 packages (10 ounces each) frozen whole kernel corn, cooked and
    drained
Salt and freshly ground white pepper to taste
8 large cooked artichokes

In a large skillet, sauté bacon until crisp, then remove and drain. Add green pepper and onion to skillet and sauté until just tender. Stir in corn, salt, and pepper. Heat thoroughly. Fill the artichokes with this mixture and top with bacon. Serve at once.

Serves: 8

Quick California Takes

Tangerines or Mandarin Oranges

Peel tangerines or mandarin oranges and separate into segments. Cut each segment in half and stir into tuna or chicken salad. Adds a special tang to cole slaw, too.

Vegetarian Curry

½ pound new potatoes or baking potato, cut into ¾-inch cubes, and cooked
¼ pound green beans, cut into 2-inch lengths, and cooked
2 medium carrots, pared, cut into thin diagonal slices, and cooked
1 cup plain yogurt
1 tablespoon all-purpose flour
1 teaspoon curry powder
½ teaspoon salt
½ teaspoon ground dried coriander
½ teaspoon ground dried cumin
½ cup flaked coconut
2 hard-cooked eggs, chopped
¼ cup skinned peanuts
3 green onions or scallions, chopped
½ cup seedless raisins

Combine potatoes, green beans, and carrots and reserve.

Mix yogurt with flour, curry powder, salt, coriander, and cumin. Stir yogurt mixture into vegetables and spoon into a saucepan. Place over low heat and heat through, stirring often. Do not boil. Turn into serving bowl and top with coconut. Place chopped eggs, peanuts, green onion, and raisins in individual dishes and serve with curry.

Serves: 4

Cabbage and Nuts

1 cup walnut halves or large pieces
3 tablespoons butter
3 cups finely shredded red cabbage
2 cups sliced, peeled, and cored apples
1 bay leaf
¼ teaspoon salt
¼ teaspoon freshly ground black pepper
¼ cup dark brown sugar, firmly packed
1 tablespoon freshly squeezed lemon juice

Drop walnuts into enough boiling water to cover, and cook 3 minutes. Drain. Spread walnuts on a baking sheet, and bake in a preheated 350° oven for 10 minutes, or until lightly browned. Remove from oven and cool.

Melt butter in a heavy skillet. Add cabbage, apples, bay leaf, salt, and pepper. Cover and cook over low heat for 15 minutes, or until cabbage is wilted. Add sugar, lemon juice, and toasted walnuts.

Serves: 4–6

Vegetable Pâté

5 large tomatoes, peeled, seeded, and diced
1 tablespoon tomato paste
2 tablespoons cornstarch
1 cup crème fraîche
9 eggs
1½ cups cooked chopped spinach
½ teaspoon freshly grated nutmeg
½ teaspoon freshly ground black pepper
Salt to taste
1 tablespoon butter
1 cup grated Gruyère cheese

Place tomatoes in a saucepan and cook over medium heat until most of the tomato juices have evaporated, and there remains approximately 1 cup of tomato pulp. Stir in tomato paste, combining thoroughly. Reserve.

Combine cornstarch and crème fraîche. Blend until smooth.

Beat eggs with seasonings, and then combine with cornstarch-crème fraîche mixture until thoroughly blended.

Using 1 tablespoon of butter, grease a 6-cup ovenproof loaf pan and lightly butter a sheet of waxed paper cut to fit the bottom of the pan. Line the pan with the waxed paper.

Add ⅓ of the egg mixture to the chopped spinach and pour into the pan, evening it out. Place the pan in a larger baking pan and place both pans on the middle rack in a preheated 300° oven. Pour boiling water into the larger pan. Water should come halfway up the sides of the loaf pan. Bake for 40 to 50 minutes, or until set.

Remove loaf pan from the oven. Combine half the remaining egg mixture with the tomatoes. Spoon over spinach layer and bake for 40 to 50 minutes, or until tomato layer is set.

Remove loaf pan from oven and combine cheese with remaining egg mixture. Spoon over tomato layer and bake for 40 to 50 minutes, or until this top layer is set.

Allow pâté to cool, and then refrigerate overnight.

Before serving, turn pâté out of loaf pan onto a serving platter. Remove waxed paper and slice.

Serves: 8–10

Quick California Takes

Crème Fraîche

To make crème fraîche, combine ½ pint sour cream with 1 pint heavy sweet cream (whipping cream). Mix thoroughly in a saucepan and heat—do not simmer—very gently. Pour cream into a container, cover partially, and allow to remain unrefrigerated overnight. By morning the cream will be thick. Stir, and refrigerate until needed.

Stir-Fried Vegetables and Fruit

1 tablespoon vegetable oil
2 small crookneck squash (about ½ pound), sliced thin
2 small zucchini squash (about ½ pound), sliced thin
1 small onion, cut into very thin wedges
1 small clove garlic, minced or pressed
½ cup bean sprouts
1 teaspoon dried thyme, crumbled
1 teaspoon soy sauce
2 medium nectarines, cut into bite-size chunks

Heat oil in a large skillet or wok. Add squash, zucchini, onion, garlic, bean sprouts, thyme, and soy sauce. Sauté over medium heat for 6 to 7 minutes, stirring, or until tender-crisp. Add nectarines. Heat through, stirring.

Serves: 6

Quick California Takes

Thinning Thoughts:
Two Dips for Raw Vegetables

In a food processor or blender, blend 1 cup cream-style cottage cheese and 2 cubed avocados until smooth.

Add ¼ cup freshly squeezed lemon juice, 1 small onion, 1 teaspoon salt, and a dash of cayenne. Blend thoroughly. Spoon into serving dish and chill.

Only 47 calories per tablespoon and great with cauliflowerets and cherry tomatoes.

In a food processor or blender, purée 2 cubed avocados until smooth. Add 1⅓ cups low-fat yogurt, 4 teaspoons freshly-squeezed lemon juice, 1½ teaspoons salt, ¼ teaspoon ground cumin, and ⅛ teaspoon hot pepper sauce. Blend thoroughly.

Only 15 calories per tablespoon. Serve with carrot and celery sticks.

Tabouli with Plums

1 cup bulgur (cracked wheat)
1½ cups boiling water
1¼ teaspoons salt
½ cup chopped green onion or scallions
½ cup diced seeded tomatoes
¼ cup chopped parsley
3 tablespoons freshly squeezed lemon juice
1¼ teaspoons dried mint, crumbled fine
½ teaspoon dried basil, crumbled
⅛ teaspoon white pepper
1½ cups sliced firm ripe plums
1 tablespoon olive oil
Lettuce leaves
Lemon wedges
Cherry tomatoes
Parsley sprigs

Combine bulgur, boiling water, and ¾ teaspoon of the salt in mixing bowl. Stir lightly; let stand until cool. Add onions, tomatoes, parsley, lemon juice, herbs, remaining ½ teaspoon salt, and pepper. Cover and chill. Shortly before serving toss with sliced plums and olive oil, mixing lightly. Serve on bed of lettuce leaves, garnished with lemon wedges, cherry tomatoes, and parsley.

Serves: 5–6

Green's Restaurant at Ft. Mason

A stylish vegetarian restaurant that serves elegant food and wine in a romantic atmosphere, Green's is run by a Zen community. This combination is something that could only happen in California. Green's is owned by a Zen Center affiliated with the Tassajara Monastery in the Carmel Valley.

For some years Tassajara has opened its doors during summer months to guests who yearned to spend a few days in a beautiful country setting. For a very small sum they're offered quiet cabins and delicious vegetarian meals prepared by Zen students who learn to cook by doing.

The Tassajara varieties of whole-grain breads were missed by the guests when they left the monastery, and there was such a clamor for their baked goods that Tassajara opened a bakery in San Francisco.

But the bread wasn't enough, and visitors kept telling the Zen group how much they missed the food they had enjoyed at Tassajara. After much discussion, the Zen community realized that opening a restaurant would be an excellent way to keep their monastery self-supporting while serving the kind of meals they believed in: vegetarian, but vegetarian with imagination. The result is Green's restaurant, and everything about it is unique. The restaurant is housed in what was once an old Army warehouse. It still looks like a warehouse from the outside, but when you walk in, you feel as though you've entered another world.

Some of the banquettes are made of redwood burl root. Chunks of redwood that look like freeform sculpture decorate the restaurant. Every table has a beautiful flower arrangement, and these are not a few posies stuck into dime-store vases, but true, Japanese-style displays of cut flowers.

An entire wall of windows looks out over one of those views for which San Francisco is famous: a marina, the Bay, and the Golden Gate Bridge beyond.

The staff at Green's are all members of the Zen community, and it is obvious they care about the guests and take pride in the food they serve. Fruits and vegetables are always fresh, organically grown, and often come from the Zen Center's Green Gulch Farm.

The head chef is a young woman, Deborah Madison, who worked with Alice Waters at Chez Panisse. Among the innovative dishes served at Green's are Marinated Tofu and Vegetable Brochette cooked over a mesquite fire, Eggplant Custard with Mushrooms, Tassajara bread grilled with olive oil, sprinkled with rosemary, sage, and sea salt, Shitake mushrooms and Grilled Tofu, cooked with wine and crème fraîche and served with fresh pasta, Chinese Noodle Salad in Ginger Dressing with cucumber, mung sprouts, tofu, and cilantro, and Poached Apricots, Figs, and Pears in a Ginger Syrup.

The wine is considered as seriously as the food, and Green's has a committee of experts to choose the wines that will go best with their unique vegetarian cuisine.

"We try to be of service to people by creating a place where they can relax," says Ed Brown, the restaurant's manager. "Green's is an outgrowth of our meditation and our life together that expresses Buddhism and Buddhist practice."

"When people enjoy our meals we enjoy that," said Chef Madison. "If food is underdone or overdone or cold, we'll throw it out rather than serve it. The food has to be right, and if what we do pleases people, it pleases us."

With all the care and creativity in evidence at Green's, the Zen community has still managed to keep lunch and dinner prices down. It's no wonder that reservations for dinner must be made weeks in advance.

Marinated Tofu and Vegetables on Skewers in the Manner of Green's Restaurant in San Francisco

Green's restaurant in San Francisco is an example of how Californians take oriental dishes and turn them into something uniquely American. Bland tofu, a soybean cake, is marinated to give it flavor, and is then cooked on a skewer over mesquite charcoal imported from Mexico. If mesquite charcoal is not available, you can cook this dish over ordinary charcoal or in a broiler.

1 ounce dried Japanese mushrooms, simmered in 1¼ cups water for 20 minutes
2 cups dry red wine
1 cup soy sauce
1 teaspoon dried marjoram
1 teaspoon ground cloves
1 clove garlic, minced
½ teaspoon freshly ground black pepper
1¼ cups olive oil
12 2-inch cubes firm tofu
2 green peppers, seeded and cut in half
2 yams or sweet potatoes, cut in ½-inch slices
2 tomatoes, quartered
2 small zuccihini, cut in 2-inch pieces
4 large mushroom caps
1 tablespoon wine vinegar
¼ teaspoon dried thyme
1 clove garlic, pressed

Combine mushrooms and the water in which they were cooked with wine, soy sauce, marjoram, ground cloves, minced garlic, black pepper, and 1 cup of the olive oil in a saucepan and cook, stirring, until the mixture comes to a boil.

Press excess water from tofu, and place in a shallow pan. Pour the hot marinade over the tofu. Cover and refrigerate for 24 hours.

Allowing 1 skewer per person, divide tofu and vegetables and thread on 4 to 6 skewers.

Combine remaining ¼ cup olive oil, vinegar, thyme, and pressed garlic and mix thoroughly. Brush this vinaigrette over tofu and vegetables on the skewers, then grill on a barbecue or in a broiler. Turn brochettes to brown evenly on all sides.

When vegetables and tofu are browned and hot, about 10 minutes, remove from heat. Serve with rice. At Green's this dish is served with brown rice.

Serves: 4–6

Fettuccine with Zucchini-Almond Sauce

3 tablespoons butter
1 pound zucchini (about 3 cups), diced
1 cup finely chopped onion
1 clove garlic, minced or pressed
2 cups tomato sauce
½ teaspoon dried oregano
¼ teaspoon red pepper flakes (optional)
¼ teaspoon dried rosemary, crushed
1 teaspoon sugar
½ teaspoon salt
1 pound fettucine noodles
¾ cup toasted slivered blanched almonds

Melt butter in a saucepan. Add zucchini, onion, and garlic. Cook until zucchini is just tender. Add tomato sauce and all seasonings. Bring to a simmer and cook, stirring occasionally, for about 10 minutes, or until all ingredients are hot and thoroughly combined.

Cook fettuccine noodles until they are *al dente,* or slightly firm.

Spoon zucchini mixture over fettuccine noodles and top with almonds.

Serves: 4–6

Easy Artichoke-Tomato Salad with Tarragon Dressing

1 jar (6 ounces) artichoke hearts
5 cups torn endive or romaine lettuce leaves
2 fresh tomatoes, cut into wedges
Tarragon Dressing (below)

Drain artichoke hearts; reserve liquid for dressing. Combine artichoke hearts, lettuce, and tomatoes.

Tarragon Dressing

Olive oil
Artichoke liquid
¼ cup tarragon vinegar
1 clove garlic, minced or pressed
½ teaspoon basil, crushed
¼ teaspoon salt
Dash of freshly ground black pepper

Add enough oil to reserved artichoke liquid to measure ⅓ cup. Combine with remaining ingredients in a bowl and stir until thoroughly mixed. Pour dressing over salad ingredients and toss gently.

Serves: 4–6

The Brown Derby's Cobb Salad

Cobb Salad is an old Hollywood tradition. The presentation is beautiful, as the individual ingredients are chopped fine and arranged on a platter in colorful rows, and shown to the guests before being tossed together. The dressing is the old-fashioned American version of French vinaigrette, calling for sugar, and salad oil rather than olive oil. This dish can be a luncheon meal, or may be served at a brunch.

1 head iceberg lettuce, finely chopped
1 bunch watercress, finely chopped
2 avocados, chopped
2 hard-cooked eggs, finely chopped
6 green onions or scallions, finely chopped
2 tomatoes, chopped

3 cups chopped cooked breast of chicken
8 slices bacon, fried, drained, and crumbled
3 ounces Roquefort cheese, crumbled
1½ cups salad oil
½ cup white vinegar
1 tablespoon freshly squeezed lemon juice
½ teaspoon freshly ground black pepper
½ teaspoon dry mustard
1 teaspoon Worcestershire sauce
1 clove garlic, pressed
½ teaspoon salt
1 teaspoon sugar

Combine lettuce and watercress thoroughly. Spread this mixture on the bottom of a large, flat-bottomed salad bowl or serving dish.

Arrange rows of avocados, eggs, green onions, tomatoes, chicken, and bacon on top of lettuce mixture. Sprinkle crumbled cheese on top.

Place all other ingredients in a jar or bowl and shake or mix thoroughly. Spoon half the dressing over the salad.

Present the dish at the table, then toss with remaining salad dressing.

Serves: 6–8

Ghirardelli Square Fruit and Nut Salad

½ cup sliced dried apricots
2 tablespoons dry white wine
¼ cup vegetable oil
1 tablespoon freshly squeezed lemon juice
1 teaspoon honey
1 teaspoon mustard
¼ teaspoon *herbe de provence* (optional)
⅛ teaspoon curry powder
⅛ teaspoon salt
1 quart shredded iceberg, romaine, or red-leaf lettuce
½ cup alfalfa sprouts
¼ cup thinly sliced sweet red onion
⅔ cup toasted walnut pieces

Combine apricots and wine. Let stand until part of wine is absorbed, stirring occasionally.

Prepare dressing by combining vegetable oil and all seasonings in a bowl and mixing thoroughly.

In a large salad bowl, toss lettuce, alfalfa sprouts, and onion, combining well. Top with apricots and toasted walnuts and pour dressing over all ingredients. Toss gently to mix and serve at once.

Serves: 4

Guacamole: The Big Debate

How many ways are there to prepare guacamole? Almost as many ways as there are cooks. Here are three versions, but guacamole is easily adapted to suit individual tastes, and as long as smooth, buttery avocado is the main ingredient, go ahead and improvise; you can't go wrong.

Guacamole I

2 large ripe avocados, peeled and pitted
1½ teaspoons minced onion
1 teaspoon freshly squeezed lemon juice
1 clove garlic, pressed
Salt and freshly ground black pepper to taste
¼ teaspoon hot pepper sauce

Purée avocados in a food processor or blender. Add all other ingredients, and process just to combine.

Yield: 2 cups, approximately

Guacamole II

2 large ripe avocados, peeled, pitted, and cut into chunks
1 clove garlic
1 small onion
2 teaspoons lemon juice
¼ teaspoon hot pepper sauce (or ½ hot chili pepper, fresh or canned)
Salt to taste
½ cup mayonnaise
1 medium tomato, chopped

Place all ingredients except mayonnaise and tomato in a food processor or blender and purée coarse. This may also be done in a food mill.

Add mayonnaise and process or stir, just to blend. Spoon guacamole into a serving dish and garnish with chopped tomato.

Yield: 2 cups, approximately

Richard Condon's Guacamole

3 medium avocados, not too ripe, peeled, pitted, and chopped
1 medium onion, chopped
2 tomatoes, peeled and chopped
2 green chili peppers (may be canned *serrano* or *jalapeño* chili peppers) chopped fine
2 tablespoons chopped fresh coriander *(cilantro)*, or a pinch of ground coriander
Salt to taste

Combine all ingredients thoroughly except salt. Bury avocado pits in guacamole and add salt just before serving. Author Richard Condon explains that these techniques prevent guacamole from discoloring.

Yield: 2½ cups, approximately

Mushroom Salad in Avocado

As the main course for a light lunch, or an interesting addition to a buffet table, serve raw, sliced mushrooms heaped into avocado halves.

3 avocados
4 hard-cooked egg yolks, finely chopped
4 tablespoons finely minced white or green onion or scallions
4 teaspoons minced fresh parsley
4 tablespoons olive oil
1 tablespoon red wine vinegar
Salt and freshly ground black pepper to taste
1 pound sliced mushrooms
4 lettuce leaves

Cut avocados in half lengthwise, remove pit, and peel. Chop 1 avocado fine. Combine with egg yolks. Add onion, parsley, oil, vinegar, and salt and pepper and blend well.

Add mushrooms and mix thoroughly. Place remaining 4 avocado halves on lettuce leaves and fill each with mushroom mixture.

Serves: 4

Mushroom-Spinach Salad with Almonds in Parmesan Dressing

¼ pound mushrooms, sliced
Parmesan Dressing (below)
4 cups torn spinach, packed
¾ cup slivered, blanched almonds, toasted
⅓ cup sliced green onion or scallions

Marinate mushrooms in Parmesan Dressing for 2 to 3 hours. Just before serving, combine spinach, almonds, and onion. Toss with mushrooms and dressing.

Parmesan Dressing

½ cup white wine vinegar or raspberry vinegar
½ cup olive oil
3 tablespoons grated Parmesan cheese
1 teaspoon dried basil, crushed
1 clove garlic, minced or pressed
¼ teaspoon salt
⅛ teaspoon freshly ground black pepper

Place all ingredients in a bowl and mix thoroughly.

Serves: 4

Blackeye Peas and Artichoke Heart Salad

1 pound blackeye peas
1 medium onion, studded with 2 cloves
1 clove garlic
2 teaspoons salt
6 black peppercorns
2 jars (4 or 5 ounces each) marinated artichoke hearts, undrained
½ cup sliced radishes
1 cup thinly sliced celery
½ cup sliced green onion or scallions
8 tablespoons olive oil
2 tablespoons wine vinegar
Salt and freshly ground black pepper
Romaine or iceberg lettuce leaves

Wash and sort blackeye peas. Combine in a large pot with six cups of water. Bring to a boil, and cook for 3 minutes. Remove from heat, cover, and let stand for 1 hour.

Add onion, garlic, salt, and peppercorns to the pot and simmer gently for about 2 hours, or until peas are tender.

Drain, discard onion and garlic, and allow peas to cool.

Add artichoke hearts with their marinade to peas. Add all other vegetables and combine.

Blend olive oil and wine vinegar thoroughly. Pour dressing over pea-vegetable mixture and toss to combine. Season with salt and pepper to taste, and serve on lettuce leaves.

Serves: 8

The 7 California Fish Story: On the Light Side, Fish and Shellfish

Sophie Porter

In California, most of the fish consumed has the name Pacific in the title, as: Pacific snapper, Pacific cod, Pacific sole, Pacific sand dab, Pacific halibut, and Pacific salmon.

This is to distinguish West Coast fish from similarly named East Coast or European fish. Pacific snapper should not be confused with red snapper; it is a variety of rockfish. And Pacific cod, also called true cod on the West Coast, can be compared to Atlantic cod in taste and texture.

Pacific sole, sand dabs, and halibut are all part of the flounder family, and one of the most popular of western soles is Petrale sole, served frequently in San Francisco restaurants.

Fresh yellowfin tuna steaks are flown in from Hawaii, and are usually sautéed or grilled, and served with an herb or fruit butter. Tuna sushi is a favorite in Japanese restaurants, and fresh tuna is a far cry from the canned version.

Salmon is popular in California, whether fresh, smoked, or canned. Pacific salmon has a lower fat content than Atlantic salmon, and while there are approximately 25 varieties of salmon, there are mainly 5 that are offered commercially. If you've ever wondered about the differences in salmon, and canned salmon can be especially confusing, here's the salmon story:

The largest salmon is called king, chinook, or spring salmon. It is marketed fileted or cut into steaks, and is also smoked.

Next comes sockeye, also known as red or blueback salmon. Sockeye is deep red in color, oily, and generally used for canning.

Silver salmon, which also goes under the names of coho or medium red, can usually be found in fish stores whole for poaching or cut into steaks. Silver salmon is also canned.

Pink salmon, ranging in color from light to deep pink, is the smallest of all salmon. It is drier than other salmon varieties, and is usually canned.

Chum or silver brite salmon is even lighter in color than pink salmon and is not oily. Chum is caught only in August and September, and may be salted or kippered.

All fish is high in protein, and calorie counts depend on the richness of the fish. Pacific cod or Pacific sole each contain 80 calories in a 3½-ounce portion, but a 4-ounce portion of fresh salmon can range anywhere from 239 calories for king salmon to 154 calories for pink salmon.

Smoked salmon has approximately the same amount of calories, according to the United States Department of Agriculture, about 50 calories per ounce.

Both smoked salmon and smoked salmon trout (so named because it is a pink-fleshed trout) are popular on the West Coast and are served as a first course.

Conscious as they are of looking and feeling good, Californians eat a lot of fish. While it is high in protein, fish is lower in fat and calories than most meats. Fish fillets or steaks may be simply grilled or broiled, and then served with a piquant flavored butter; many fish dishes are prepared with an unusual sauce that includes fruit or nuts.

In addition to fish, Californians eat a wide and wild variety of shellfood. Grey snails, called *petit-gris* in France, are now raised on good California lettuce and spinach, and may be served in a cream sauce studded with pink peppercorns or combined with sweetbreads in a white wine sauce, topped with puff pastry. Sea urchins, limpets from Hawaii, spiny Pacific lobster, squid or calamari, Dungeness crabs, tiny Bay shrimp, large Monterey prawns, Bay oysters, crayfish, mussels, and abalone, are all familiar foods on the West Coast, as are a myriad of dishes prepared with Alaska King crab.

These giant crabs from icy Alaskan waters can weigh as much as 25 pounds, and can measure as much as six feet from claw tip to claw tip. (By comparison, Dungeness crabs caught in California's northern waters are six-and-a-half inches across.) King crab takes well to freezing, so it's available year 'round on the West Coast as well as across the rest of the country. It can be prepared as simply or as elaborately as the restaurant or home chef wishes, and a favorite California first course is made with King crab legs, split, and served with lemon and butter. In addition to ease of preparation, King crab is also popular because a 3-ounce serving contains lots of minerals, Niacin, Vitamin A, and only 81 calories. And for a bright smile, say some Californians, the natural fluoride in crab just may help prevent tooth decay.

Fresno Baked Fish Fillets

Petrale sole, seen frequently on California menus, is rarely seen elsewhere around the country. Petrale sole is a species of flounder, so any flounder or sole fillet may be used in this recipe.

1 cup pitted ripe olives (black California olives), drained and chopped
1 medium tomato, seeded and finely chopped
½ cup finely minced carrots
1½ teaspoons dried thyme, crumbled
Freshly ground black pepper to taste
½ cup minced fresh parsley
4 petrale sole, flounder, or sole fillets (about 1½ pounds)
2 tablespoons butter
1 cup packed fresh parsley sprigs
⅓ cup sour cream
1 clove garlic
4 leaves fresh basil (or 1 tablespoon dried basil)
1 lemon, sliced

Combine olives, tomato, carrots, thyme, pepper, and the minced parsley. Spoon equal amounts down the center of the fish fillets. Roll fish around filling and place seam side down in a shallow, 1½-quart baking dish well greased with the 2 tablespoons of butter. Cover and bake in a preheated 400° oven for 25 minutes, or until fish flakes easily.

While fish is cooking, prepare sauce: combine parsley sprigs with sour cream, garlic, and basil in a food processor or blender, and purée. Spoon into a saucepan and heat gently until warm. Do not boil. To serve, spoon sauce over the fish and garnish with lemon slices.

Serves: 4

Baked Fish Fillets with Clams and Grapes

4 fish fillets or fish steaks (sole, halibut, or flounder)
2 tablespoons butter
Salt and freshly ground black pepper to taste
1 small onion, minced
1 can (7¼ ounces) minced clams, undrained
2 cups seedless grapes
1 lime, thinly sliced
½ cup dry white wine
2 tablespoons chopped fresh parsley

Place fish in a shallow, lightly greased baking dish. Dot with butter and season with salt and pepper.

Combine onion, clams, and clam juice and spoon over fish.

Combine grapes, lime, and wine and spoon over fish.

Bake in a preheated 400° oven for 10 minutes, or until fish flakes easily. Garnish with chopped parsley

Serves: 4

Fish Tacos

Tacos are Mexican, and Pacific snapper is one of California's favorite fish; put them together and you have a good example of the way West Coast folks take other cuisines and make them uniquely their own. You can start from scratch and cook fish just for this dish, but it is a perfect way to use leftover fish fillets.

1 onion, chopped
4 tablespoons vegetable oil
1 cup tomato sauce
2 small jalapeño peppers (fresh or canned), rinsed, seeded, and
    chopped
2 cups chopped cooked fillets of fish (Pacific snapper, perch, sole or
    flounder)
8 corn tortillas (or packaged taco shells)
2 cups Guacamole I or II (see page 68)
½ cup sour cream
8 tablespoons grated Monterey Jack or Cheddar cheese
8 tablespoons shredded lettuce
2 tomatoes, chopped

In a skillet, sauté onion in 1 tablespoon of the oil, stirring until onion is wilted, but not brown. Add tomato sauce and jalapeño peppers to skillet, and stir to combine. Cover and cook over low heat for 5 minutes.

Add fish to tomato-pepper mixture, and cook for 3 to 5 minutes, or until all ingredients are hot.

Heat remaining 3 tablespoons of oil in a small skillet and add tortillas one at a time, and cook briefly, turning once. As tortillas are removed from oil they will be limp. Shape each tortilla into a folded shell, and cook in skillet until crisp. The tortilla has now become a taco. Drain on paper towels.

Fill each taco shell with fish, and top with guacamole and sour cream.

Serve each taco garnished with grated cheese, lettuce, and tomatoes.

Serves: 4

Halibut with Walnuts in Foil

2 halibut steaks (about 2 pounds)
Salt and freshly ground black pepper to taste
3 tablespoons freshly squeezed lemon juice
1¼ cups finely chopped walnuts
⅔ cup grated sharp Cheddar cheese
¼ cup milk
2 tablespoons melted butter
½ cup bread crumbs

Place the fish on a well-buttered sheet of heavy duty aluminum foil. Sprinkle with salt, pepper, and lemon juice.

Combine walnuts, cheese, and milk to make a paste. Spread over the top of the fish. Combine butter and bread crumbs and spread on nut paste. Wrap the fish in the foil and place on a grill, about 3 inches from hot coals, or bake in a preheated 400° oven.

Grill or bake for 35 minutes. Slit top of foil to allow steam to escape, and continue baking until fish flakes easily.

Serves: 4

Salmon Steaks with Garlic Confit

Can there be such a thing as too much garlic? The following recipe calls for 16 cloves prepared as confit or preserves, but do not let it frighten you. The longer it's cooked, the more gentle garlic becomes. Fish baked with garlic confit will offend no one.

16 large cloves garlic
Vegetable oil, goose fat, or clarified butter
1 small bay leaf
¾ teaspoon dried marjoram
¼ teaspoon dried thyme
1 inch piece orange peel
1 inch piece lime peel
1 small tomato, peeled and diced
1 tablespoon chopped parsley
4 pieces baking parchment or aluminum foil (about 12 × 8 inches each)
4 salmon steaks, about 1 inch thick, approximately 2 pounds (or cod, bass, or halibut steaks)
Salt
4 tablespoons butter
Lemon wedges
2 tomatoes, sliced

Peel garlic and place in a very small saucepan. Pour on enough oil, goose fat, or clarified butter to cover. Add bay leaf, ¼ teaspoon of the marjoram, and the thyme. Simmer gently over very low heat for 30 minutes, making sure the garlic does not brown. Remove from heat and allow to cool. You now have garlic confit.*

---

* Garlic confit can also be served with roast chicken, loin of pork, or leg of lamb.

Pour boiling water over orange and lime peel, let stand a minute, drain, cut in half, and combine with tomato, parsley, and remaining ½ teaspoon marjoram.

Brush parchment or foil with the oil in which garlic was cooked, and slice 1 clove garlic onto each sheet. Place a fish steak on the garlic, sprinkle with salt, and slice a second garlic clove for top of each steak. Sprinkle each steak with ¼ of the tomato-herb mixture, and top each with 1 tablespoon butter. Fold parchment or foil over fish, and fold edges together, sealing tightly. Place packets in a shallow baking pan.

Bake in a preheated 450° oven for about 15 minutes, or until fish flakes. To serve, open package, and garnish each fish steak with 2 cloves garlic confit, lemon wedges, and slices of tomato.

Serves: 4

Salmon Sausalito

2 firm ripe Bartlett pears
4 tablespoons butter
½ teaspoon salt
½ teaspoon dry mustard
¼ teaspoon dried basil, crumbled
2 tablespoons chopped, fresh, dillweed
⅛ teaspoon herb pepper seasoning
1 chicken bouillon cube, crumbled
1 cup thinly sliced onion
1 cup julienne cut carrot
4 1-inch-thick salmon steaks, about 2 pounds (sea bass or other firm
      fish may be used)
2 small tomatoes, peeled and sliced
1 lemon, thinly sliced

Halve, core, and quarter the pears. Melt 2 tablespoons of the butter and mix with salt, mustard, basil, dillweed, and herb pepper. Pour over pears and reserve.

Melt remaining 2 tablespoons of butter in a large skillet. Add bouillon cube, onion, and carrot; mix thoroughly. Cook slowly, covered, for 5 to 10 minutes.

Add fish steaks, pears with butter mixture, and tomato and lemon slices. Cover and cook for 10 minutes, or until fish flakes easily with a fork.

Serves: 4

Quick California Takes

With Kiwi Fruit:

Skewer 1 large, cooked, peeled, and deveined shrimp with 1 wedge of peeled kiwi fruit on a fancy cocktail pick, and serve with drinks before dinner.

Mirassou Vineyards Seafood Terrine

As made on the West Coast, this recipe calls for fillets of Pacific snapper (not to be confused with Red Snapper). Pacific snapper is a variety of rock fish, and if it is not available, tilefish or monkfish makes a fine substitute.

⅓ cup chopped shallots
4 tablespoons butter
2 tablespoons all-purpose flour
½ cup dry white wine
1 pound boned Pacific snapper fillets, cut into large cubes
½ pound shelled cooked small shrimp
2 teaspoons fresh tarragon (or 1 teaspoon dried)
3 large eggs
½ teaspoon salt
¼ teaspoon freshly ground white pepper
1 cup heavy sweet cream (whipping cream)
½ pound skinned boneless salmon fillet

In a small pan, sauté shallots in butter until soft and translucent. Add flour and cook, stirring, over medium heat for 3 minutes. Add wine and continue cooking and stirring another 3 minutes, or until mixture becomes a thick paste. Cool.

Place snapper, shrimp, and tarragon in a food processor and process to a smooth purée. Add shallot mixture, eggs, salt, and pepper and process until well blended. With processor running, slowly add the cream and process only until well blended.

Butter a 4½ x 8½-inch loaf pan or terrine. Cut salmon fillet into 2 strips of equal size. Spoon half the fish purée into the mold. Arrange the salmon strips end to end down the center, and top with remaining fish purée. Smooth down the top, and cover with buttered foil.

Place terrine in a larger pan, and add boiling water until it reaches halfway up the sides of the terrine. Bake in a preheated 350° oven for 30 minutes, or until a knife inserted in the center of the terrine comes out clean. Allow to cool, and refrigerate until well chilled, at least 4 hours.

Serve with *Sauce Verte.* (see below)

Serves: 6–8

Sauce Verte

2 cups mayonnaise
1 tablespoon lemon juice
1 tablespoon fresh tarragon
1 tablespoon rinsed and chopped anchovies
1 tablespoon chopped chives
¼ cup parsley sprigs
1 cup tender spinach leaves or fresh sorrel
Salt and freshly ground white pepper to taste

Place all ingredients in food processor or blender and process until sauce is smooth. Refrigerate.

Yield: 2½ cups, approximately

Nyda's Snapper and Spinach

This recipe was created by Nyda Delegeane of the Delegeane Garlic Farms in Yountville, California. If Pacific snapper is not available, this dish can be prepared with red snapper, flounder, or tilefish fillets. Nyda recommends that this dish be prepared a day in advance to give the flavors a chance to blend.

3–4 pounds Pacific snapper fillets
Salt and freshly ground black pepper to taste
4–6 tablespoons olive oil
4–6 tablespoons butter
2 pounds spinach, chopped
4 medium potatoes, peeled and quartered
1 medium onion, minced

2 cloves Elephant Garlic, minced (or 1 clove garlic, pressed)
1 cup stewed tomatoes
1 cup tomato sauce
¾ cup dry white wine
1 tablespoon fresh chopped parsley
1 teaspoon fresh chopped basil

Cut fillets into 2- or 3-inch pieces, and season with salt and pepper. Heat 1 tablespoon oil and 1 tablespoon butter in a large skillet. Cook the fish over medium heat until lightly browned, adding 1 or 2 tablespoons each of oil and butter as needed. Reserve.

Cook spinach for 2 minutes. Drain and reserve.

Boil potatoes in salted water until tender. Drain and reserve.

Heat 2 tablespoons each of oil and butter in a skillet. Sauté onion until lightly browned. Reduce heat to low; add garlic. Cook 4 minutes. Add stewed tomatoes, tomato sauce, and wine. Simmer 5 minutes. Add parsley and basil.

Spoon a thin layer of tomato mixture over the bottom of an ovenproof casserole. Place alternate pieces of fish and potatoes in casserole. Top with half the cooked spinach and half the tomato mixture. Repeat with remainder of spinach and the tomato mixture. Bake in preheated 350° oven for 30 minutes. If serving on the following day, reheat for 15 to 20 minutes in a preheated 350° oven.

Serves: 6–8

The Classical Influence

There are many elegant French restaurants on the West Coast that emphasize classic French cuisine. How does this traditional feasting fit in with California cuisine? It becomes a happy blend of European techniques combined with the fine foods of California, and it's a style of cooking that's quite popular among the show business folk of southern California, and the bankers of northern California. One of the places where it is found is the L'Escoffier Restaurant atop the Beverly Hilton Hotel in Los Angeles. The Beverly Hilton was the late Conrad Hilton's flagship hotel, and the restaurant is proof that a large hotel can serve fine food if it is inspired to do so.

The inspiration here comes from Auguste Escoffier, revered as the king of cooks, and the cook of kings, and it is taken very seriously by Steven

Martin, director of food and beverage operations at the hotel. Steven Martin is so insistent that the L'Escoffier remain true to tradition that he removed onion soup from the menu when a food writer insisted that in Escoffier's day onion soup would have been served in the kitchen to the help, never in front of the house to the guests.

Working with him to keep faith with Escoffier is Raymond Dreyfus, Chef de Cuisine. Chef Dreyfus is especially proud of the dinner he created to honor the 135th birthday celebration of Auguste Escoffier.

The recipes were Escoffier's best, and many of the ingredients were California's best, as was evident in the menu:

Le Consommé à la Vigneronne—clear beef broth with seedless grapes
Les Paillettes d'Or—golden cheese straws
La Truite en Filet Caruso—fillet of rainbow trout with lobster mousse and white wine sauce
Le Tournedos Maréchale—fillet steak with fresh asparagus
La Barquette aux Trois Purées—patty shell with puréed vegetables
La Salade de Laitue à la Huile de Noix—limestone lettuce with walnut oil dressing
Le Camembert Frit—fried Camembert cheese wedges
La Pêche Melba—ice cream and peach dessert created in 1894 for opera star Nellie Melba

Escoffier would have loved the dinner, and he would have enjoyed the grapes, peaches, lettuce, and other California products that contributed to this splendid meal.

Truite en Chemise à la Restaurant L'Escoffier

Truite en Chemise can mean trout baked in a pastry crust, but Californians who are diet conscious prefer their trout wrapped in spinach leaves. (Especially since the sauce is laden with butter and cream.) This recipe can also be prepared with fillet of sole or flounder.

12 fillets of fresh trout
Salt and freshly ground black pepper to taste
24 large washed spinach leaves
4 tablespoons butter
4 shallots, chopped fine
1 cup dry white vermouth
1 cup dry white wine
2 tablespoons butter, melted
½ cup heavy sweet cream (whipping cream)

Season trout fillets with salt and pepper. Wrap each fillet in 2 spinach leaves and reserve.

In an oven-proof dish heat the 4 tablespoons of butter. Add shallots and cook, stirring, for 3 minutes. Add vermouth and wine, and heat until ingredients are warm and well combined.

Place spinach-wrapped fish fillets in dish, and place dish in a preheated 400° oven. Cook for 10 to 15 minutes, by which time the liquid should be reduced.

Remove dish from oven. Place fish fillets on a warm serving dish, and add melted butter and cream to juices in baking dish. Heat on top of stove for 30 seconds, or until all ingredients are thoroughly combined, and pour over fish fillets.

Serves: 6

Architect and Chef: Jeremiah Tower

Jeremiah Tower was an architect before he began working with Alice Waters at her restaurant, Chez Panisse. That was in the early seventies when Chez Panisse had just opened, and as Jeremiah said, the inventive but non-professional chefs weren't quite sure what each night's dinner would bring.

Sometimes the supplies Alice ordered didn't show up, and sometimes what did show up wasn't good enough by Chez Panisse standards. Many dishes were invented on the spot an hour or so before they were served, and the one person who understood the quantity of food needed in a restaurant would indicate a spot high up on a large pot and say, "Make soup up to here."

Recently, Jeremiah Tower presided over an inexpensive and unassuming restaurant in a quiet corner of San Francisco. If you wandered into the Balboa Cafe and didn't know enough to ask for a menu, you might eat a good enough hamburger, but if you took a look at the menu, Jeremiah's influence was evident.

The Balboa Cafe offered appetizers of Black Forest ham with melon and nicoise olives, carpaccio with mustard sauce, limestone lettuce with hazelnut oil vinaigrette, and smoked trout with watercress and walnut salad.

The pasta dishes included fettucine with fresh tomatoes, and a lemon, basil, and cream sauce, and fettucine with avocado and cream. There was also a fine main dish of grilled albacore tuna with orange and basil butter.

While Jeremiah worked at the Balboa Cafe he was also completing plans to open his own restaurant near the San Francisco opera house. The emphasis would be on a return to true bourgeois cooking, with guests experiencing the earthiness of a bubbling casserole or steaming marmite brought directly to the table. Jeremiah also planned to prepare dishes *sur command* where guests could order something special 24 hours in advance.

Bourgeois cooking? As in French bourgeois cooking, Jeremiah was asked? Jeremiah hoped to combine the best of two worlds: French regional cooking and American regional cooking, using the bounty of California. Monterey prawns, squab, quail, Pigeon Point oysters, a Cream of Corn soup with Crayfish Butter were all to be served at _____?

"Well," said Jeremiah, "it will probably be called 'Jeremiah's.'"

Broiled Tuna Steaks with Orange Butter à la Jeremiah Tower

4 tablespoons olive oil
Juice of ½ lemon
4 1-inch-thick tuna steaks* (about ½ pound each)
Freshly ground black pepper to taste
6 tablespoons butter, softened
2 tablespoons orange juice
1 teaspoon grated orange peel

Combine olive oil and lemon juice and brush tuna steaks with mixture. Season with black pepper. Reserve.

Prepare orange butter by combining butter, orange juice, and orange peel. Mash until all ingredients are thoroughly combined. Reserve.

Place tuna steaks in a preheated broiler or an outdoor grill and broil for 5 minutes on one side. Turn and cook an additional 5 to 10 minutes, or until fish flakes.

Remove to a serving platter, and garnish with orange butter.

Serves: 4

*Fresh tuna appears on California menus often, sometimes listed as "albacore." If tuna is not available, swordfish or mako steaks may be substituted.

Phil Paladino's Quick Ziti and Tuna

Phil is a Hollywood press agent-publicist, with a Hollywood press agent's flair and flamboyance. Every now and again he takes over the kitchen in his Bel Air home to whip up a pot of ziti and tuna. The more people drop in, the happier Phil is, adding quantities of olive oil and tuna to a huge, 9-quart pot.

"This'll feed a cast of thousands," he announces, as people come into the kitchen to taste the bubbling sauce, "let's invite some more people over!"

1 cup olive oil
2 large onions, chopped
2 large green peppers, chopped
3 cloves garlic, minced
Salt and freshly ground black pepper to taste
½ teaspoon dried basil
¼ teaspoon dried thyme
¼ teaspoon hot pepper sauce
3 cans (6 ounces each) tomato paste
8 cans (6 ounces each) water
3 cans (about 7¾ ounces each) tuna, drained
2½ pounds ziti, cooked *al dente*

Pour olive oil into a large pot. (Phil says: "Do not use a frying pan.") Add onions, peppers, garlic, and all seasonings and cook until onions are almost black. (Says Phil.)

Add tomato paste and water, and stir to combine all ingredients thoroughly. Bring to a simmer and cook for 10 minutes.

Add tuna and simmer gently for an additional 30 minutes, stirring occasionally.

If you're using a large enough pot, spoon cooked ziti directly into it, and serve from the pot. Or spoon ziti into a large serving platter, and pour sauce over the pasta, and toss before serving.

Serves: 10–12

Crab-Stuffed Artichokes

Serve Crab-Stuffed Artichokes as a main course after a first course of soup. Follow with a rich dessert for a meal that combines the ying and yang of two fairly low-calorie courses with a finale to make all dessert-loving guests happy.

4 large artichokes
1 tablespoon butter
2 tablespoons all-purpose flour
½ cup dry white wine
½ cup heavy sweet cream (whipping cream)
1 cup cooked crab meat, cartilage removed
⅛ teaspoon hot pepper sauce
¼ teaspoon Worcestershire sauce
Salt and freshly ground white pepper to taste
½ cup bread crumbs mixed with 1 tablespoon melted butter

Wash artichokes, and using a sharp knife, remove stalk and about ½ inch of the tops of the leaves. Trim off tough, outer leaves around the bottoms of each artichoke.

Place artichokes in a saucepan with enough water to almost cover the artichokes. Cover, and cook until tender, about 1 hour.

Remove artichokes from saucepan, invert on a board or plate, and drain thoroughly.

After artichokes have cooled, turn right side up and gently pull open the center leaves. Pull out a few of the center leaves, leaving a small space to hold the stuffing.

Melt butter in a saucepan, add flour, and cook, stirring constantly, for 3 minutes. Add wine and cream, stirring constantly. Add hot pepper sauce, Worcestershire sauce, and salt and pepper. Simmer for 5 minutes. Add crab meat and simmer for an additional 3 minutes, stirring. Allow mixture to cool, then stuff artichokes. Top with bread crumb-butter mixture.

Bake artichokes in a preheated 350° oven about 10 minutes, or until crumb topping is lightly browned. Serve hot.

Serves: 4

Crab and Vegetables Orientale

1½ teaspoons cornstarch
½ teaspoon sugar
1 tablespoon cold water
1 teaspoon soy sauce
1 teaspoon dry sherry wine
3 tablespoons oil
½ teaspoon salt
1 package (10–12 oz.) frozen split Alaska King crab legs, thawed
⅓ cup chicken broth
½ cup thinly sliced water chestnuts
½ large onion, sliced
2 small celery stalks, cut in ¼-inch slices
1 cup fresh or frozen Chinese pea pods or sliced broccoli flowerets

Combine cornstarch with sugar and gradually blend in water, soy sauce, and sherry. Reserve. Heat oil in wok or large skillet, add salt and crab. Stir, and cook for 2 minutes.

Add broth and vegetables and cook, covered, for 5 minutes. Remove cover, add cornstarch mixture, and cook, stirring, for 1 minute or until slightly thickened.

Serves: 2

Aquaculturists: Mats and Dafne Engstrom

It doesn't take long for new arrivals to adopt the California spirit of "let's try it, let's do it." Mats and Dafne Engstrom are the Swedish-born proprietors of a company aptly named California Sunshine. Formed in 1974, California Sunshine was established in order to supply northern Europe with crayfish. Crayfish, known as crawfish in Louisiana, is much loved in the Scandinavian countries, and it abounds in the Sacramento and San Joaquin rivers.

The Engstroms harvested the crayfish, and shipped them both live and frozen in a dill brine to Scandinavia. While working on their growing crayfish business, the Engstroms became interested in caviar. They discovered that there were sturgeon swimming in California waters, and that sportfishermen who caught the fish threw the roe away. The Engstroms decided to learn all they could about how to turn sturgeon roe into proper caviar, and today, in conjunction with the University of California at Davis, they are researching the possibility of garnering sturgeon roe by Caesarean section, thus saving the life of the fish.

Sturgeon caviar is great, and California Sunshine does produce a small amount of this American caviar. But the Engstroms have developed a new product that gladdens the heart of caviar lovers who are not yet millionaires.

The product worth cheering about is called American Golden Caviar, and it comes from the more common whitefish rather than the rarer sturgeon. Whitefish caviar was available before Golden Caviar arrived on the scene, but it tasted less than wonderful. It was dyed black and heavily salted. American Golden Caviar, marketed under the Tsar Nicoulai label, has a natural and delicate golden apricot color. There are no added colors or preservatives. The flavor is mild, not salty, and the caviar is flash frozen after processing so that the taste is fresh, not fishy. Golden Caviar can be kept in a freezer for a year, and it may be defrosted and then refrozen.

The price fluctuates according to supply, but it is approximately one-tenth the price of imported sturgeon caviar. Californians who love the good life loved American Golden Caviar the moment it became available, and it quickly appeared on the menus of the Stanford Court and Chez Panisse in San Francisco and Ma Maison and Michael's in Los Angeles, stuffed lavishly in new potatoes, spooned over pasta, and sprinkled on oysters.

The Engstroms don't limit themselves to crayfish and caviar, however. Their smoked salmon trout is processed over a wood fire with never a nitrite or nitrate around, and they're currently working on a process to cold-smoke King Salmon which they say will be different and better than any smoked salmon on the market.

Spinach Pasta & Scallops with Golden Caviar

1 pound scallops (leave small bay scallops whole, cut large sea scal-
     lops in half)
Salt and freshly ground black pepper to taste
2 tablespoons butter
½ cup dry white wine
4 tablespoons heavy sweet cream (whipping cream)
4 tablespoons mayonnaise
4 tablespoons olive oil
1 tablespoon white vinegar
2 tablespoons chopped fresh basil
½ pound spinach pasta, cooked *al dente*
4 ounces Golden Caviar

Rinse scallops and pat dry with paper towels. Season with salt and pepper.

Combine butter and wine in a skillet. When hot, add scallops and cook quickly, turning to cook on all sides. Scallops will be done in 3 or 4 minutes. Remove from skillet and reserve.

Add cream to skillet and cook, stirring, for 2 minutes, or until all ingredients are thoroughly combined and mixture has thickened slightly. Remove from heat and allow to cool.

Combine mayonnaise with oil and vinegar and beat until thoroughly mixed. Stir in cream mixture and add basil.

Combine half the cream sauce with the cooked pasta and toss.

Combine remainder of sauce with scallops and mix.

Spoon pasta on a serving plate. Top with scallops, and spoon caviar over scallops. This dish is served at room temperature.

Serves: 4

Seafood Crêpes

½ cup mashed avocado
4 eggs
½ cup all-purpose flour
¼ teaspoon salt
½ cup milk
1–2 tablespoons water
Butter to cook crêpes
6 tablespoons butter
3 tablespoons all-purpose flour
½ cups milk, heated
½ cup diced Swiss cheese
½ teaspoon Worcestershire sauce
Salt and freshly ground black pepper to taste
1 pound small shrimp, cooked and cleaned
½ cup grated Swiss cheese

Combine avocado, eggs, flour, salt, milk, and water. Using a food processor, blender, or whisk, blend until mixture is smooth.

Using a small non-stick skillet or crêpe pan, heat butter and cook crêpes over medium heat, turning once. Reserve cooked crêpes.

Melt 2 tablespoons of the butter in a saucepan and stir in flour. Gradually add hot milk, stirring constantly, and cook until sauce begins to thicken. Add diced cheese and continue cooking until cheese melts.

Remove from heat and stir in Worcestershire sauce, salt, and pepper. Fold in shrimp.

Place a portion of the sauce and shrimp on each crêpe and fold.

Arrange crêpes in a single layer in a well-greased baking dish. Sprinkle with grated cheese and dot with remaining 4 tablespoons of butter. Bake in a preheated 400° oven for 10 to 15 minutes, or until crêpes are hot and cheese is melted.

Serves: 4–6

Monterey Artichokes with Shrimp and Lemon Sauce

6 egg yolks
½ cup chicken stock or broth
½ cup heavy sweet cream (whipping cream)
2 tablespoons dry white wine
2 tablespoons freshly squeezed lemon juice
2 teaspoons minced fresh tarragon (or ½ teaspoon dried)
Salt and freshly ground white pepper to taste
6 large artichokes, cooked, with leaves trimmed and choke removed
1 pound small shrimp, cooked and cleaned

Combine all ingredients except artichokes and shrimp in top of a double boiler over barely simmering water. Whisk until mixture thickens and doubles in volume, about 3 minutes. Reserve and keep warm.

Place each artichoke on individual serving plates. Open leaves slightly and, dividing shrimp evenly, fill the centers. Spoon warm Lemon Sauce over the artichokes.

Serves: 6

Shrimp Curry Pacifica

1 cup seedless grapes
½ cup finely chopped onion
2 tablespoons butter
¼ cup all-purpose flour
2 cups chicken broth
¼ cup dry white wine
1 tablespoon curry powder
1 teaspoon salt
1 pound cooked large shrimp, shelled and deveined
1 tablespoon freshly squeezed lemon juice
Hot cooked rice

Purée grapes in a food processor or blender. Reserve.

Sauté onion in butter in large saucepan over low heat until limp. Stir in flour; gradually add broth. Add grape purée, wine, curry powder, and salt. Stir over low heat for about 10 minutes, or until sauce thickens.

Add shrimp and lemon juice; heat thoroughly.

Serve with rice and curry accompaniments, such as shredded coconut, peanuts, chutney, and raisins.

Serves: 4

Shrimp with Garlic Butter

¼ pound butter
2 tablespoons finely chopped parsley
4 teaspoons finely chopped shallots
4 cloves garlic, finely chopped
¼ teaspoon paprika
⅛ teaspoon cayenne pepper
⅛ teaspoon salt
2 teaspoons Pernod
½ teaspoon freshly squeezed lemon juice
1½ pounds large shrimp, shelled and deveined
All-purpose flour, enough to coat shrimp lightly
⅓ cup olive oil
Juice of ½ lemon
¾ cup dry white wine

Cream butter for a couple of minutes with a wooden spoon. Add the next 8 ingredients (up to the shrimp) and blend well.

Flour the shrimp lightly. Heat the oil in a large skillet. Shake the excess flour from the shrimp and add them to the skillet. Sauté shrimp very quickly, for about 3 minutes over medium-high heat. As soon as they start to color, turn them to the other side. When shrimp are cooked, add lemon and wine, and stir briefly for about 1 minute. Add the garlic butter to pan and toss the shrimp around quickly in the butter. When butter is melted, serve the shrimp immediately.

Serves: 6

Squid Abalonetti

Squid, also known as calamari, is a popular California seafood, and Abalonetti's Restaurant in Monterey offers it a variety of ways. Their most popular dish is the following deep fried squid combined with eggplant and served with a spaghetti sauce.

2 pounds squid, cleaned, cut open into flat pieces, and then into 2-inch squares
½ cup evaporated milk
1 egg, beaten
Salt and freshly ground black pepper to taste
1 cup cracker meal
Vegetable oil for frying
2 tablespoons butter, softened
1 eggplant, peeled, sliced, and fried
2 cups spaghetti or marinara sauce

Pat the squid dry. Combine milk, egg, salt, and pepper. Beat until thoroughly mixed. Dip squid pieces into milk-egg mixture, and then roll in cracker meal.

Heat oil in a large skillet and fry squid pieces in a single layer for 3 to 4 minutes. Turn to brown on all sides, but do not overcook, or squid will toughen. Drain squid on a paper towel and reserve.

Butter a 12 × 8 × 2-inch baking dish with the softened butter. Arrange a layer of eggplant slices in the dish. Top with squid, and pour spaghetti or marinara sauce over all.

Bake in a preheated 350° oven for 10 to 15 minutes, or until all ingredients are heated through.

Serves: 4

Bouillabaisse West Coast Style

3 medium onions, sliced
1 large green pepper, sliced
2 cloves garlic, pressed
4 cups stewed tomatoes
1 leek, white part only, chopped
1 carrot, sliced and parboiled
2 celery stalks, sliced
8 mushrooms, sliced
6 tablespoons olive oil
1 can (6 ounces) tomato paste
2 tablespoons anchovy paste
2 tablespoons chili sauce
1 tablespoon freshly squeezed lemon juice
1 teaspoon dried thyme
1 teaspoon dried fennel seeds
Pinch of saffron
Freshly ground black pepper to taste
1 tablespoon salt, or to taste
½ cup dry white or red wine
4–5 pounds mixed fish and shellfish, cut in large chunks (may be
    combination of cod, eel, halibut, perch, prawns, scallops, lob-
    ster, clams, etc.)

In a large bowl, combine onions, green pepper, garlic, stewed tomatoes, leek, carrot, and celery.

Sauté mushrooms in 2 tablespoons of the oil, stirring, for 5 minutes,
and add to vegetable mixture.

In a large saucepan, combine tomato paste, anchovy paste, remaining
4 tablespoons of olive oil, chili sauce, lemon juice, thyme, fennel,
saffron, pepper, salt, and wine. Mix thoroughly, and add the vegetable
mixture.

Bring to a boil. Lower heat and simmer rapidly for 10 minutes to allow
the liquid to reduce. Cover and simmer for 15 minutes more. Let cool
and refrigerate overnight.

Before serving, heat sauce to a boil. Turn heat down until sauce
simmers, and add combined fish and shellfish. Cover and cook for 15
minutes, or until all fish is cooked.

Serves: 8–10

Fisherman's Wharf Fish Stew

4 tablespoons olive oil
4 tablespoons butter
1 large onion, chopped
2 cloves garlic, pressed
8 tomatoes, peeled and chopped, or 4 cups canned Italian plum
      tomatoes
1 can (6 ounces) tomato paste
1 green pepper, chopped
½ teaspoon dried oregano
½ teaspoon dried basil
1 bay leaf
¼ teaspoon red pepper flakes, crushed
3 cups dry red or white wine
2 pounds fish, cut into large pieces (may be sea bass, Pacific snap-
      per, red snapper, Pacific ling cod, Eastern cod, or halibut, or a
      combination)
½ pound scallops
½ pound medium shrimp, shelled and deveined
12–15 clams, unshelled, thoroughly scrubbed
1 fresh Dungeness crab, cracked (or 10–12 ounces frozen Alaska
      King crab split legs, thawed)

Heat oil and butter in a large pot or Dutch oven. Sauté onion and
garlic, stirring, for 3 minutes, or until onion is wilted.

Add tomatoes and tomato paste, and cook, stirring, until all ingredients
are warm. Add green pepper, seasonings and wine, stir to combine,
and cover. Simmer over low heat for 30 minutes.

Add the fish, and cook for 15 minutes. Add shellfish, and cook for an
additional 10 to 15 minutes, or until all the fish is cooked, and clams
have opened. Correct seasoning and serve at once.

Serves: 8–10

Sophie Porter

Meats and 8 Poultry: Prepared in New, Ethnic, Classic and Traditional Ways

It's rarely plain broiled-steak-for-dinner in California. Meats may be spiced or combined with fruits, and ordinary dishes are transformed by ideas that stem from a variety of origins: some ethnic, and others classic, but most are the result of breezy, Californian imagination.

The metamorphosis of braised short ribs is an example. Around the rest of the country, braised short ribs are an inexpensive, not very elegant beef dish, but in California short ribs are prepared according to a Korean recipe, and have become party fare.

And then there's roast lamb that is spice-cured before roasting, pork gussied up with a kiwi fruit sauce, chicken aromatic with an abundance of Elephant Garlic—all new flavor combinations meant to make meat entrées very special.

Beef Chimichangas

1 pound ground beef
1 medium onion, chopped
3 tablespoons vegetable oil
1 cup refried beans (homemade or canned)
1 medium tomato, peeled and chopped
2 tablespoons Mexican hot sauce (homemade or canned salsa
       jalapeño)
1 teaspoon dried oregano
½ teaspoon dried cumin
Vegetable oil
8 burritos (wheat flour tortillas)
1 cup grated Monterey Jack or Cheddar cheese
Shredded lettuce
Sour cream (optional)

Heat the oil and sauté beef and onion over high heat for 10 to 15 minutes, or until beef is cooked. Remove from heat. Combine with beans, tomato, sauce, oregano, and cumin.

Oil a skillet lightly and fry each tortilla until it begins to crisp. Drain on paper towels. Spoon some of the filling into the center of each tortilla and roll up.

Heat 1 to 1½ inches oil in a skillet. Fry chimichangas until golden. This will take about 2 minutes. Remove from oil and drain on paper towels. Top with cheese and lettuce, and sour cream, if desired.

Serves: 4

Korean Cuisine California Style

Driving from downtown Los Angeles to Beverly Hills on Olympic Boulevard, Korean signs and Korean restaurants are everywhere. But the restaurants have a West Coast twist, and the signs say: "Korean Barbecue" and "Korean Fish and Chips." Despite the Americanization, the restaurants also serve authentic Korean dishes, and next to the take-out Japanese sushi bars, the takeout Korean restaurants are coming along fast as the new and popular ethnic food. Many Korean dishes are made with inexpensive cuts of beef. Short ribs are a special favorite, and Korean-style barbecued beef ribs are an interesting change from the usual pork spareribs.

Korean Beef Barbeque

4   pounds beef short ribs, cut into slices, or cut lengthwise
        (sometimes labeled as flanken)
1   cup soy sauce
2   tablespoons sugar
4   cloves garlic, minced
1-inch piece fresh ginger, minced
6   green onions or scallions, chopped
¼   cup sesame oil
2   tablespoons sesame seeds
½   teaspoon hot pepper sauce

Place ribs in a large bowl. Combine all other ingredients, and pour over ribs. Cover and refrigerate for 8 hours, or overnight.

Barbecue over coals or roast meat in a preheated 400° oven, turning from time to time, and basting with marinade. Cook until meat is tender, approximately 30 minutes.

Serves: 6

Braised Beef Ribs Korean

4 pounds beef short ribs, cut into 2- to 3-inch pieces
4 cups water
½ cup soy sauce
3 tablespoons sugar
2 garlic cloves, minced
½-inch piece fresh ginger, minced
2 tablespoons sesame seeds
½ teaspoon hot pepper sauce or hot pepper oil
2 carrots, sliced
2 eggs
1 tablespoon all-purpose flour
½ cup water
Vegetable oil to cook crêpes

In a large pot or Dutch oven, combine the beef and 4 cups of water. Add soy sauce, sugar, garlic, ginger, sesame seeds, and hot pepper sauce or oil. Stir to combine, and bring to a boil. Cover, lower heat, and simmer until meat is tender, approximately 2 to 3 hours.

Add carrots and simmer an additional 20 minutes, or until carrots are tender.

Combine eggs, flour, and ½ cup of water and beat to mix thoroughly. Heat a small amount of oil in a skillet, crêpe pan, or omelet pan and cook egg mixture the way you would cook crêpes.

When crêpes have cooled slightly, cut into ¼-inch strips and reserve.

Spoon cooked ribs and sauce on a large serving platter, and garnish with crêpe strips.

Serves: 6

Slivered Steak Tartare from Korea

¾ pound lean boneless beef (top round or sirloin)
2 tablespoons soy sauce
1 tablespoon sugar
1 thin slice fresh ginger, minced
1 garlic clove, minced
1 tablespoon sesame seeds, toasted
2 green onions or scallions, chopped
1 teaspoon hot pepper sauce

1 small firm pear
2 tablespoons freshly squeezed lemon juice
1 egg yolk
1 cup shredded cabbage
1 cup shredded carrot

Trim meat of all fat. Cut meat across the grain into ¼-inch slices, and then cut slices into thin slivers.

Combine soy sauce, sugar, ginger, garlic, sesame seeds, scallions, and hot pepper sauce. Mix thoroughly, add to meat, and stir to blend well. Cover and refrigerate for 2 hours.

Peel pear, and cut into thin lengthwise slices. Cut each slice in half. Toss pear slices with lemon juice. Reserve.

To serve, place meat slivers on a platter. Create a well in the center, and place egg yolk in well. Toss meat with egg yolk, mixing thoroughly. Serve meat slivers with pear, cabbage, and carrots as accompaniments in separate bowls.

Serves: 2–3

Quick California Takes

Homemade Garlic Salt:

Peel 1 clove Elephant Garlic and add to ½ cup salt. Transfer to a jar. Close tightly, and let stand for 3 days. Remove and save garlic, and use salt as needed.

Garlic Toast:

Not to be confused with garlic bread. Toast rye or black bread slices. Rub garlic clove on both sides of bread slices. Place a pat of butter in between bread slices. Wrap bread in foil and heat in a preheated 350° oven for 15 minutes before serving.

Flank Steak with Pears

3 Bartlett pears
1 flank steak (1¾–2 pounds)
¼ cup dry white wine
3 tablespoons soy sauce
3 tablespoons vegetable oil
½ teaspoon freshly ground black pepper
½ teaspoon dried thyme
2 teaspoons ground ginger

Peel and core the pears, then cut into thick slices. Place pear slices in a shallow dish with the steak. Combine remaining ingredients and pour over pears and steak. Marinate in refrigerator for 2 hours, turning steak, and spooning marinade over steak and pears several times.

Place steak and pears in a broiler pan. Brush with marinade. Broil 4 to 5 minutes; then, brush with marinade, and broil 5 minutes longer.

Cut steak into thin, diagonal slices. Garnish with pear slices.

Serves: 6

Lamb Kebabs with Figs

½ cup pineapple juice
¼ cup soy sauce
2 tablespoons brown sugar
¼ teaspoon ground ginger
⅛ teaspoon garlic salt
1½ pounds leg of lamb, cubed
6 slices bacon, cut in half crosswise
12 pineapple chunks
12 dried Calimyrna figs

Combine pineapple juice with soy sauce, brown sugar, ginger and garlic salt.

Make kebabs by combining alternately on skewers: lamb, bacon, pineapple, and dried figs.

Place kebabs in a shallow pan, pour pineapple marinade over all, and refrigerate for several hours. Drain kebabs, reserving marinade. Broil for 20 minutes, turning once and brushing with marinade. Serve with hot rice.

Serves: 6

Sacramento Stuffed Steak

1 cup cooked spinach, drained
1 cup pitted ripe olives (black California olives), sliced
1 tablespoon minced onion
1 clove garlic, pressed
¼ teaspoon freshly ground black pepper
1 egg, beaten
1 flank steak (about 2 pounds)
4 tablespoons vegetable oil
½ cup dry sherry wine
1 cup sour cream

Combine spinach, ½ cup of the olives, onion, garlic, pepper, and egg, mix thoroughly and spread on steak, leaving a 1-inch margin all around. Roll up lengthwise and tie with string.

Heat oil in a Dutch oven and brown meat all over. Pour sherry over meat. Cover and simmer 15 to 20 minutes, or until meat is tender; remove steak to a warm platter.

Add sour cream and remaining ½ cup of olives to Dutch oven and heat gently. Slice meat and spoon sauce over all.

Serves: 6–8

Kiwi Fruit

Until recently, most kiwi fruit was shipped to the United States from New Zealand. Now California grows kiwi fruit, and this delicate green fruit that originated in China's Yangtze Valley is available in most parts of the United States.

When kiwi fruit was shipped in from New Zealand it was used sparingly in fruit tarts, but now that it's in good supply, Californians use it generously in appetizers and main dishes.

Lamb with Kiwi Fruit Sauce

An inexpensive cut of lamb can be festive with the addition of kiwi fruit. If you've won a lottery or a horse race, however, this dish can also be prepared with rib or loin lamb chops.

1 tablespoon vegetable oil
4 shoulder lamb chops, trimmed
2 cloves garlic, minced
Salt and freshly ground black pepper to taste
¼ cup port wine
½ cup beef broth
1 tablespoon grated orange peel
2 kiwi fruit, peeled and sliced thin
2 tablespoons butter

Heat oil in a large skillet and brown lamb chops over high heat, turning to brown both sides. Lower heat and add garlic, salt, and pepper to chops. Cover chops and cook until tender, approximately 20 to 30 minutes, depending on quality of meat. Remove chops from skillet and reserve.

Add wine, broth, and orange peel to skillet, and cook, stirring constantly, over high heat until sauce reduces. Return chops to skillet, and add kiwi fruit. Lower heat to medium high and cook for 1 minute.

Serves: 4

Lamb in Mushroom Cream Sauce

10 tablespoons butter
4 cups sliced mushrooms
3 bay leaves
2 teaspoons Worcestershire sauce
½ cup brandy
4 cups heavy sweet cream (whipping cream)
Salt to taste
⅛ teaspoon white pepper
3 pounds loin lamb, cut into sixteen medallions
¼ cup dry white wine
2 tablespoons minced fresh chives

Heat 5 tablespoons of the butter in a skillet. Add mushrooms and bay leaves and cook over medium-high heat, stirring frequently, for 10 minutes. Add the Worcestershire sauce.

Pour the brandy over the mushrooms, ignite, and shake the pan constantly until the flames are extinguished. Add the cream and cook over low heat, stirring often, until the cream has reduced and thickened. Add salt and pepper and reserve.

In another skillet, heat the remaining 5 tablespoons of butter. When butter is hot, add the meat and quickly sear it until just done, about 2 minutes on each side; do not overcook. Transfer meat to a warm plate.

Over high heat, add wine to a skillet and deglaze the pan, stirring and scraping the bits from the bottom. Add the mushroom sauce to the pan juices and heat thoroughly. Stir in the chives. Add the medallions of lamb and heat thoroughly.

Serves: 8

Rack of Lamb with Sauce Paloise

2 racks of lamb (8 small chops on each rack)
2 tablespoons butter
Salt and freshly ground black pepper to taste

Have the butcher trim most of the fat from the racks of lamb, and ask him to French the ends of the chops, removing the fat from the rib ends of the bones, so that each bone end can be seen individually.

Score the fat on the racks of lamb. Spread 1 tablespoon of butter on top of each rack. Season, then place the racks in a shallow baking pan. Roast in a preheated 425° oven for 30 minutes. Lamb should be crispy and brown on top, and pink within.

Slice the lamb at the table. If racks are small, figure on 4 chops per person. If racks are larger, 2 or 3 chops will be sufficient.

Serve with Sauce Paloise (below).

Serves: 4–8

Sauce Paloise

½ cup wine vinegar
½ cup dry white wine
6 shallots, chopped fine
6 tablespoons finely chopped fresh mint leaves
4 fresh basil leaves, chopped fine
6 egg yolks, beaten with 2 tablespoons water
2 cups Clarified Butter (see p. 106)
Salt and freshly ground white pepper to taste
6 teaspoons finely chopped fresh mint leaves

Combine vinegar, wine, shallots, 5 tablespoons of the mint leaves, and basil in a saucepan. Bring to a boil, and cook for 5 to 10 minutes to reduce. Allow to cool.

Add beaten egg yolks to the sauce and stir to combine.

Using a double boiler or a heavy saucepan, cook sauce over low heat, whisking or whipping constantly until mixture thickens. Off heat, stir in clarified butter, and add seasoning.

Strain sauce, and stir in remaining mint leaves. Sauce should be kept warm, but should not be allowed to simmer.

Yield: 2½ cups, approximately

Quick California Takes

Clarified Butter

To clarify butter: Place butter in a heavy saucepan. Allow to melt over very low heat. Do not stir. Spoon off the clear, golden butter on top, leaving the white residue at the bottom of the pot. The clear liquid is clarified butter, and it can be spooned into a jar, refrigerated, and stored for months.

Sonoma County Spice-Cured Rack of Lamb

1 rack of lamb (8 chops)
2 cloves garlic, minced
2 shallots, minced
2 green onions or scallions, minced
1 teaspoon Chinese Five-Spice Powder
½ teaspoon ground Szechuan pepper
2 sprigs fresh rosemary (or ½ teaspoon dried rosemary)
2–3 pounds lamb bones
Salt to taste

Trim fat carefully from lamb and reserve. Fat should be cut in thin sheets from top of rack of lamb.

Combine garlic, shallots, green onions, and spices. Mix thoroughly, and rub this dry marinade into lamb. Press rosemary sprigs into lamb.

Place reserved sheets of fat over lamb, and tie fat over the meat with string.

Wrap meat in plastic wrap, and place in refrigerator for 4 days. Meat will be cured by that time.

One day before lamb is to be served, prepare a stock by roasting lamb bones in a shallow pan in a preheated 450° oven for 20 to 30 minutes, or until bones are well browned.

Place browned bones in a pot, cover with water, and simmer for 4 hours. Degrease and strain liquid, and reduce until you have 1 to 1½ cups liquid. Add salt to taste.

Bring the rack of lamb to room temperature. Remove extra fat, and scrape off most of the marinade.

Place lamb in a shallow baking pan, and roast in a preheated 450° oven for 20 minutes for rare lamb, 30 minutes for medium rare. This lamb is best served rare.

Heat reserved lamb stock, and spoon over roast lamb.

Serves: 2–4

Chalupa

1 pound pinto beans, washed and sorted
Pork roast (3 pounds)
7 cups water
½ cup chopped onion
2 cloves garlic, minced
1 tablespoon salt (or to taste)
2 tablespoons chili powder
1 tablespoon dried cumin
1 teaspoon dried oregano
1 (4 ounce) can green chili peppers, chopped
Tortillas

Put all ingredients except tortillas in a Dutch oven or crock pot. Cover and simmer about 5 hours, or until roast falls apart and beans are tender. Uncover and cook an additional 30 minutes.

Serve with tortillas and, if you wish, with such accompaniments as chopped tomato, chopped avocado, chopped onion, shredded lettuce, grated Cheddar cheese, and spicy taco sauce.

Serves: 8

Cowboy Bean and Ham Stew

This savory stew featuring ham and beans borrows its robust seasonings from the chuck wagon cooks of the old western cattle ranges. The secret is long, slow cooking and your electric slow cooker is ideal for the job. Just follow the directions that come with your particular model. If you don't have an electric slow cooker you can slow cook the stew over very low heat in a heavy pot with a tight lid.

1 pound pinto beans or Great Northern beans
1 ham hock or shank
1 large onion, chopped
6 cups water
1 teaspoon salt
1 can (7–10 ounces) green chili salsa
2 cups stewed tomatoes.

Rinse and sort beans. Combine all ingredients in a large pot. Cover and heat to boiling.

Reduce heat and simmer gently. Keep the pot covered and add enough boiling water as necessary to keep beans well covered. Cook until beans are tender and meat is done, approximately 3 hours.

When beans are done, remove ham bone, cut off the meat, and return the meat to the pot. Serve the stew hot with corn bread.

Serves: 6

Lichee Pork Chops with Almonds

4 center-cut loin pork chops, about 1–1½ inches thick
Salt and freshly ground black pepper to taste
2 tablespoons vegetable oil
½ cup chicken broth
⅓ cup blanched and slivered almonds, toasted
½ cup snow pea pods
½ cup canned lichees (do not use dried lichees)
¼ cup syrup from lichees
3 tablespoons brandy

Season pork chops with salt and pepper. Heat oil in a large skillet and sear chops on each side over medium-high heat. Reduce heat, and drain fat from skillet.

Add chicken broth to chops in skillet. Cover and cook for 20 to 30 minutes, or until chops are well done. Mix almonds, pea pods, lichees, and syrup and spoon around pork chops. Heat for 2 minutes.

Pour brandy over chops and ignite. Spoon flaming pan juices over chops carefully until flames burn out. Serve chops with cooked rice or buckwheat pasta cooked *al dente*.

Serves: 3–4

Sage-Flavored Pork Chops with Kiwi Fruit Sauce

2 tablespoons olive oil
4 center-cut loin pork chops, about 1 inch thick
2 cloves garlic, peeled and left whole
Freshly ground black pepper to taste
6 fresh sage leaves (or ½ teaspoon dried sage)
1 bay leaf
½ cup orange juice
4 kiwi fruit, peeled and coarsely chopped
⅓ cup dry vermouth
Salt to taste

Heat olive oil in a large skillet and brown pork chops on both sides over medium-high heat. Lower heat and add garlic, pepper, sage, and bay leaf to pan. Cover and cook until pork chops are almost done, approximately 20 minutes.

Uncover chops, and remove garlic and bay leaf.

Combine orange juice, kiwi fruit, and vermouth in a bowl, and pour over chops. Cook, uncovered, until chops are well done and all sauce ingredients are thoroughly heated.

Correct seasoning and serve chops with sauce.

Serves: 2–4

Tofu-Pork Balls Rong Shing Style

1 pound tofu
½ pound lean ground pork
1 egg
2 tablespoons cornstarch
1 teaspoon soy sauce
Vegetable oil
2 tablespoons water
1 teaspoon hot pepper oil
1 tablespoon soy sauce
1 cup chicken broth
1 pound spinach
2 tablespoons vegetable oil
1 clove garlic, minced
½ teaspoon ground ginger
1 small green pepper, seeded and sliced in rounds

Press water out of tofu and mash. Combine tofu, pork, egg, 1 table-spoon of the cornstarch, and 1 teaspoon soy sauce. Mix thoroughly. Shape the mixture into 2-inch balls.

Heat 2 inches of oil in a deep skillet or wok. When oil is hot, place tofu-pork balls in pan and cook until brown on all sides. Remember that pork has to be thoroughly cooked.

Combine remaining tablespoon of cornstarch with 2 tablespoons of water. Add hot pepper oil, remaining tablespoon of soy sauce, and chicken broth. Mix thoroughly and reserve.

Wash spinach and drain. Heat 1 tablespoon of the oil in a large skillet or wok and add spinach. Stir-fry for 2 minutes, or until spinach is just wilted. Transfer spinach to a serving platter.

Add another tablespoon oil to the skillet or wok and sauté garlic and ginger, stirring constantly, for 1 minute. Add reserved chicken broth mixture to pan and cook, stirring, until sauce is thickened. Add tofu-pork balls and cook 2 more minutes, stirring frequently, until all in-gredients are hot.

Spoon tofu-pork balls and sauce over spinach. Garnish with green pepper slices.

Serves: 4

Quick California Takes

With Oranges:

Peel an orange, and scrape away white pulp from peel. Cut peel into thin strips or slivers. Dry orange peel in a slow 275° oven for 20 to 30 minutes. Cool and store in a covered jar in the pantry. A teaspoon or two of dried orange peel does amazing and wonderful things to braised or potted beef dishes, long-cooking lamb, and sauces for roast pork.

Fresh Peaches and Sausage

1 beef bouillon cube
½ cup rice
2 medium zucchini, peeled and cut into julienne strips
1 tablespoon vegetable oil
½ pound sweet Italian sausage
3 peaches, peeled and sliced
½ cup chopped parsley
½ cup sliced carrots
6 tablespoons vegetable oil
1½ tablespoons wine vinegar
1 clove garlic, pressed
Dash of freshly ground black pepper

Combine bouillon cube with 1 cup of water in a saucepan. Bring to a boil. Add rice and return to boil. Lower heat, cover, and simmer 15 to 20 minutes, or until rice is tender. Stir zucchini into hot rice, cover, and set aside.

Heat oil in a skillet and sauté sausages over medium heat for 20 to 30 minutes, or until thoroughly cooked and browned. Drain sausages, cool, and slice into thin rounds.

Combine rice mixture, sausage, peaches, parsley, and carrots and reserve.

Combine oil, vinegar, garlic, and pepper. Mix thoroughly. Spoon over rice-sausage mixture and toss, combining thoroughly. Chill until served.

Serves: 4

Marin County Polenta and Sausage

1 cup yellow cornmeal (polenta)
3½ cups water
2 teaspoons salt
1 cup grated Tillamook or Cheddar cheese
10 ounces hot Italian sausage
2 tablespoons vegetable oil
1 cup finely chopped onions
1 clove garlic, minced
1 medium-size green pepper, sliced
½ teaspoon dried thyme
1 bay leaf
¼ cup tomato sauce
2½ cups cooked plum tomatoes, chopped

Blend cornmeal with 1 cup of water. Put 2½ cups of water in a saucepan, add salt, and bring to a boil. Slowly add cornmeal mixture and cook, stirring constantly, for 10 to 15 minutes over low heat, or until cornmeal is thick and bubbly. Add cheese and stir until melted. Keep polenta warm over low heat.

Brown sausage in ½ tablespoon of the oil until sausage is thoroughly cooked. Cool slightly and cut into ½-inch slices. Reserve.

Sauté onions, garlic, and green pepper in remaining 1½ tablespoons oil until onions are translucent. Add remaining ingredients to onion mixture, and simmer, stirring frequently, for 3 minutes. Add sausage slices. Cover and cook, for 15 minutes.

Spoon warm polenta onto a serving platter and top with sausage mixture.
Serves: 4

Scalloppine of Veal with Mustard

4 tablespoons butter
4 tablespoons olive oil
1½ pounds thinly sliced veal scalloppine (about 12 slices)
½ onion, finely chopped
4 tablespoons butter
¼ pound mushrooms, finely chopped
4 tablespoons dry sherry wine
1 bay leaf
Pinch of dried rosemary

Salt to taste
Freshly ground white pepper to taste
3 cups heavy sweet cream (whipping cream)
4 tablespoons Dijon mustard
¼ cup beef stock

Heat 4 tablespoons of the butter and oil in a large skillet and quickly sauté veal slices until lightly browned. Transfer veal to a warm plate, or place in a 200° or 250° oven. Veal should be kept warm, but needs no additional cooking or it will become dry.

Sauté onion in remaining 4 tablespoons of butter. Add mushrooms and continue to sauté for 3 minutes.

Add bay leaf, rosemary, salt, and white pepper. Stir in the cream and simmer very gently until sauce is reduced by half

Stir in mustard and beef stock and return to a simmer. Remove from heat. Correct seasoning. Pour over veal slices and serve.

Serves: 6

Scalloppine with Lemon Sauce à La Stanford Court

6 tablespoons butter
2 pounds thinly sliced veal scalloppine (about 16 slices)
¼ cup lemon juice
1 tablespoon Worcestershire sauce
2 cups strong beef broth
¾ cup butter
Salt to taste

In a large skillet, heat the butter over high heat and sauté the veal, quickly searing each side until veal is lightly browned. Transfer the veal to a warm plate, or place in a 200° or 250° oven. Veal should be kept warm, but needs no additional cooking or it will become dry.

Turn the heat to medium high, and add the lemon juice, Worcestershire sauce, and broth. Stir and cook for 1 minute.

Add the butter in bits, stirring constantly. As soon as each bit of butter combines with the sauce, add more. The butter should blend into the sauce without becoming overly heated.

Remove the skillet from the heat as soon as the last bit of butter is incorporated into the sauce. Pour the sauce over the veal and serve.

Serves: 8

Jim & Nyda Delegeane and Elephant Garlic

How do you get to the Delegeane Garlic Farm? Rent a car in San Francisco and ask for a map. Trace the road to the Napa Valley and start driving. Go across the Golden Gate Bridge past Sausalito and follow the signs that say Napa. Pass Larkspur, San Rafael, and Vacaville.

The Delegeanes have told you to look for a sign that says St. Helena. That means you're on the right road because St. Helena comes after Yountville, and Yountville is where the Delegeanes live.

Go south on Route 29 and left on Madison. Turn left before the dead end, and after a short half-block turn right. Now you're on Yountville Crossroad. Go one mile over the bridge and on the left you'll see a small, gray, just-us-folks farmhouse. You know it's the Delegeanes' place because Jim and Nyda have told you that there's a red wood barn, and construction going on. If you didn't know what to look for you'd probably drive right by without meeting the Delegeanes, and without hearing the kind of success story that most people believe happened only in 19th-century novels.

Jim and Nyda were home gardeners who had jobs in the local school system. Nyda was a school nurse, Jim a school teacher. They liked garlic, so they grew it. They heard about a really mammoth garlic bulb—ten times the size of ordinary garlic—and thought it would be fun to grow that, too. They sent for seed cloves, and they grew a crop of this huge garlic. Nyda and Jim experimented in cooking with it and discovered that because its flavor was milder than regular garlic, it could be used thinly sliced or chopped to add crunch as well as flavor to fish, meat, and poultry dishes.

The following season they planted still more seed cloves, and they decided to try selling the big garlic by mail order. They named their product Elephant Garlic, and they were pleased to discover how quickly it became popular with people interested in gourmet cooking. Specialty food shops also wanted Elephant Garlic, and soon a food broker came knocking at their door offering to sell all the Elephant Garlic the Delegeanes could grow.

Nyda and Jim quit their jobs and today grow and sell Elephant Garlic, as well as regular garlic which is twisted into ropes and is a popular gift item at holiday times.

Nyda says:

Elephant Garlic lasts about 3 months, but it can last a lot longer if it is sliced or chopped, and then frozen. Baked Elephant Garlic cloves are delicious; you bake them with meat (don't peel them); after they're baked, remove the skin and spread the garlic on crackers.

Jim says:

Elephant Garlic tastes good and looks pretty while it's growing, too. Its leaves resemble those of a tulip.

Roast Chicken with Garlic Sauce

Chicken with 20 cloves of Elephant Garlic?! Yes, and as the Elephant Garlic cooks, it flavors the chicken delightfully and becomes itself a most delicate vegetable.

1 roasting chicken (3–4 pounds)
Salt and freshly ground black pepper
Sweet paprika
8 tablespoons butter
2 cups chicken stock or broth
20 whole cloves Elephant Garlic, unpeeled
1 cup dry white wine

Season chicken inside and out with salt, pepper, and paprika. Place chicken in a roasting pan. Place 4 tablespoons of butter on top of chicken, and 4 tablespoons butter in cavity.

Strew garlic cloves around chicken, and pour 1 cup of chicken stock into roasting pan.

Roast chicken in a preheated 350° oven, basting frequently, for about 1½ to 2 hours, or until tender.

When chicken is cooked remove it to a serving platter and keep warm. Remove garlic cloves and reserve.

Spoon pan juices into a saucepan. Pour wine into roasting pan and deglaze the pan over medium-high heat, scraping up bits from bottom of the pan. Add the sauce to the saucepan.

Pop the garlic cloves out of their skins by gently squeezing between fingers. Combine garlic and remaining cup of chicken broth in a food processor or blender, and purée until thoroughly smooth.

Add garlic purée to saucepan and simmer for 2 or 3 minutes, stirring frequently. When sauce is hot and all ingredients are thoroughly combined, pour sauce around chicken, or serve separately in a sauceboat.

Serves: 4–6

San Francisco Style Chinese Chicken Salad

1 chicken (2½–3 pounds), poached, or steamed for 20 minutes
Vegetable oil for frying
2 cups rice noodles (vermicelli)
½ teaspoon sesame seed oil
2 teaspoons dry mustard
3 tablespoons vegetable oil

1 teaspoon Chinese Five Spice powder
Salt to taste
3 tablespoons chopped fresh coriander
3 green onions or scallions, shredded
½ head iceberg lettuce, shredded
1½ cups cashew nuts, crushed
2 tablespoons toasted sesame seeds
Lettuce leaves

Cut chicken into 8 pieces. Heat oil in a large skillet or wok, and fry chicken pieces until completely cooked. Reserve chicken, discard oil.

Heat fresh oil in the skillet or wok, and fry noodles. Noodles will grow to two or three times their original size, so it is best to fry a handful at a time and remove from skillet to drain on paper towels. Reserve fried noodles.

Bone the chicken and cut meat and skin into fine shreds. Toss shredded chicken with sesame seed oil.

Combine mustard, 3 tablespoons vegetable oil, Five Spice Powder, and salt. Mix thoroughly. Add coriander, green onions or scallions, shredded lettuce, nuts, and sesame seeds. Mix once again. Add shredded chicken to this mixture, and combine thoroughly.

Add fried noodles to chicken mixture, and toss lightly. Serve on lettuce leaves.

Serves: 4–6

Spiced Chicken Breasts with Grapes

4 chicken breasts, skinned, boned, and halved
Freshly ground white pepper to taste
4 cups chicken broth or stock
6 sprigs parsley
4 tablespoons butter
¼ cup all-purpose flour
¾ cup milk
¼ cup dry vermouth
½ teaspoon hot pepper sauce
¼ teaspoon ground cardamom
2 cups grapes, halved and seeded

Sprinkle chicken with white pepper and reserve.

Heat chicken broth. Add parsley. When broth simmers, add chicken breasts, cover, and simmer gently until chicken is tender, about 25 minutes. Remove chicken breasts and reserve. Reserve broth.

Melt butter in a saucepan. Add flour, and cook, stirring constantly, for 1 minute. Gradually add milk, and cook, stirring until smooth.

Add 1½ cups of reserved chicken broth, stirring to combine. Add vermouth, hot pepper sauce, and cardomom. Bring to a simmer, stirring. Add grapes and cook just long enough to heat, about 30 seconds. Correct seasoning and pour sauce over chicken breasts.

Serves: 4–6

Roast Squab Chickens Stuffed with Figs and Olives

A squab chicken is a small chicken, approximately 1 pound in weight. In France these baby chickens are called *poussins*, and they are served one to a person.

In California where they are plentiful, this dish would be prepared with squab, but small squab chickens work very well, and if they're not available, you can use this stuffing quite successfully with a 2½- to 3-pound chicken.

The trick here is not to put the stuffing in the cavity of the bird, but to very carefully loosen the skin over the breast, and to place the stuffing between the skin and the breast meat. As the bird roasts it will plump up, and the stuffing keeps the breast meat exceptionally moist.

2 squab chickens, about 1 pound each (or 2½–3-pound chicken)
6 slices of the best white bread you can bake or buy, crusts removed
1 clove garlic, pressed
1 egg
¼ teaspoon freshly ground white pepper
Livers from birds, chopped
½ cup chopped dried figs
1 cup ripe olives (black California olives), finely chopped
2 tablespoons chopped fresh parsley
Salt to taste
8 tablespoons butter
1½ cups chicken broth

Very carefully, loosen skin over the breasts of the birds. Set birds aside.
In a large bowl, or using a food processor, combine bread slices, garlic,

and egg. Mix thoroughly. Filling should be moist; if it seems too dry, add another egg.

Stir in pepper, livers, figs, olives, parsley, and salt. Mix well until all ingredients are thoroughly combined.

Stuff birds between skin and breast meat, and place birds in a roasting pan that has a cover.

Place butter and chicken broth in a saucepan and heat until butter has melted. Stir to combine.

Spoon ⅓ of the broth over the birds. Cover and roast in a preheated 375° oven for 30 minutes, basting every 10 minutes.

Remove cover, baste birds with remaining broth and continue roasting, uncovered, for an additional 30 to 45 minutes, or until chickens are browned and tender.

Serves: 2, if using squab chickens; 3 if using 2½–3-pound chicken

A Hot Bird and a Cold Bottle

Squab is a popular dish in California. It's not as expensive on the West Coast as it is in much of the rest of the country, and a single squab makes an elegant main course. Squab is also used a great deal in California Chinese cooking: a special favorite is Squab Soong, which can also be made with chicken if squab is unavailable.

Because squab is not so prevalent in the rest of the United States, the recipe for Roast Squab can also be made with Rock Cornish hens or squab chickens.

Squab has a stronger flavor than chicken and Californians traditionally serve it with a red, rather than a white wine.

Roast Squab

2 squabs, Rock Cornish hens, or squab chickens
½ cup dry white wine
5 tablespoons olive oil
3 cloves garlic, minced
1 bay leaf
½ teaspoon dried thyme
4 whole cloves garlic, peeled
1 cup chicken stock or broth
1 slice onion
2 tablespoons butter
2 tablespoons brandy

Remove livers from squabs, clean, and reserve. Place birds in a shallow pan.

Combine wine, 2 tablespoons of the olive oil, minced garlic, bay leaf, and thyme. Mix well and pour over the squabs. Turn birds to coat all over, and marinate in refrigerator for several hours or overnight, turning several times.

Place whole garlic cloves and 2 tablespoons of oil in a saucepan and simmer 20 minutes over very low heat, or until garlic is soft, but not browned. In another saucepan, combine broth and onion, and simmer for 30 minutes, or until reduced to ½ cup.

Brown squab livers in 1 tablespoon of the butter. Flame with 1 tablespoon of the brandy. Purée livers and garlic cloves in a food processor or food mill. Add liver-garlic mixture to reduced broth, and reserve.

When ready to cook squabs, drain well and dry with paper towels. Heat remaining 1 tablespoon each butter and oil in an ovenproof skillet, add birds, and brown well on all sides. Drain fat from pan, add remaining tablespoon of brandy and flame. Place skillet with birds in a preheated 450° oven and roast for 30 to 45 minutes.

Heat liver-garlic sauce and serve with birds.

Serves: 2

Cheese-Stuffed Squab, Scot Horrobin Style

2 squabs
2 cups ricotta cheese
¼ pound Monterey Jack cheese, grated
2 sprigs fresh rosemary, chopped
Salt and freshly ground white pepper to taste
4 tablespoons butter, softened
8 strawberries
Lettuce leaves

Carefully loosen skin between breast and thighs of birds.

Combine cheeses and rosemary, and mix well. Season cavities of birds with salt and pepper.

Working carefully, stuff cheese mixture between skin and flesh of birds. Truss legs of squabs, and season birds on the outside. Place 1 tablespoon butter in each cavity.

Place birds in a shallow baking pan, spread remaining butter on breasts, and roast in a preheated 400° oven for 30 to 40 minutes, or until birds are tender. Baste birds every 10 minutes with pan juices.

Remove squabs and allow to cool for 15 minutes. Using poultry shears or a sharp carving knife, cut each bird in half. Cut each half into 4 pieces.

Carefully make thin, lengthwise cuts in each strawberry, up to, but not through, the stem. Gently spread the slices so each strawberry has a fan-like shape.

Place lettuce leaves on a serving platter. Arrange squab pieces on top and garnish with strawberries.

Serves: 4

Squab Soong, Mandarin Style

San Francisco's Chinatown is well known and well loved by residents and visitors alike, but one of San Francisco's truly elegant Chinese restaurants, the Mandarin, is located not in Chinatown, but on Ghirardelli Square close to Fisherman's Wharf. *Ch'ao Bai-Koh Soong* is one of the Mandarin's exquisite specialties, and the following recipe is adapted from the original and renamed Squab Soong.

1 large head iceberg lettuce
¼ pound rice noodles (vermicelli)
Vegetable oil
2 large squabs
2 green onions or scallions, white part only
12 dried black mushrooms, presoaked*
½ inch piece fresh ginger
1 cup water chestnuts
3 tablespoons sliced Virginia ham
2 tablespoons dry sherry wine
1 tablespoon oyster sauce
1 tablespoon soy sauce
½ teaspoon sugar
Pinch of salt
Pinch of white pepper
½ teaspoon sesame seed oil
2 teaspoons cornstarch dissolved in 2 tablespoons water

Separate lettuce into leaves and reserve.

In a large skillet, heat enough oil to come up about 2 inches in the pan. The rice noodles will be deep fried, and they will expand, so it is best to cook them a handful at a time.

*To prepare black mushrooms: soak in lukewarm water for 2 hours. Squeeze dry. Soak in fresh lukewarm water overnight. Drain before using.

When the oil is hot, drop a handful of noodles into the pan and cook until they are puffed. Remove noodles as they cook, and drain on paper towels.

Cut squabs into pieces, and bone. Chop meat with the skin into fine pieces and reserve.

Mince scallions and reserve. Mince mushrooms, ginger, water chestnuts, and ham.

Coat a wok or skillet with ¼ cup vegetable oil. Add squab and scallions, and stir-fry quickly. Add mushrooms, ginger, water chestnuts, and ham, and stir-fry for 2 or 3 minutes. Add all additional ingredients to the pan, and stir-fry until ingredients are heated and well combined.

Spoon over fried rice noodles and serve with iceberg lettuce leaves on the side. Tell each guest to put a tablespoonful of the squab and noodle mixture on a lettuce leaf, fold, and eat out of hand.

Serves: 4–6

Talking Turkey

California is a big producer of this big bird: 20 million turkeys annually. And West Coast turkey people are big in talking up the economic and nutritional advantages of turkey. Turkey is no longer the bird that's served only at Thanksgiving. It's available and inexpensive year 'round, and has less than half the fat of lean ground beef. A 4-ounce serving of turkey contains approximately 216 calories, and turkey can be used as a main ingredient in Mexican and Oriental cookery. Leftover turkey? Use yesterday's roast in today's soups and salads, or serve with an interesting sauce.

Turkey Cutlets Cantonese

1½ pounds turkey cutlets, cut in thin slices from breast
½ teaspoon salt
¼ teaspoon freshly ground black pepper
3 tablespoons vegetable oil
1½ tablespoons cornstarch
1½ cups chicken stock or broth
½ teaspoon ground ginger
1 teaspoon brown sugar
2 tablespoons sherry wine
1 tablespoon wine vinegar
¼ cup soy sauce
1 green pepper, seeded and sliced
1 carrot, sliced thin

Season turkey with salt and pepper. Heat oil in a skillet and cook cutlets until golden brown, turning once. Turkey cutlets cook quickly, so be careful not to overcook. Remove cutlets from pan. Combine all remaining ingredients in pan. Cook and stir until sauce clears and thickens and vegetables are tender-crisp. Return turkey to sauce and reheat.

Serve with rice.

Serves: 4

Walnut Sauce and Leftover Turkey

3 tablespoons butter
¼ cup finely chopped walnuts
3 tablespoons all-purpose flour
2 cups half-and-half (or light cream)
½ teaspoon salt
1 teaspoon Dijon mustard
¼ teaspoon grated lemon peel
½ teaspoon lemon juice
12 slices roast turkey (about 1½ pounds), warmed
14 walnut halves

Melt 1 teaspoon of the butter in a saucepan. Add chopped walnuts and sauté over low heat, stirring frequently, until lightly toasted. Remove walnuts and reserve. In the same saucepan, melt remaining butter; stir in flour and cook over low heat for 1 minute, stirring. Add half-and-half, salt, mustard, lemon peel, and lemon juice. Cook over medium heat, stirring, until sauce simmers and thickens. Remove from heat and stir in toasted walnuts.

Spoon sauce over turkey and serve with buttered noodles.

Serves: 6

Breads, 9 Quiches, Calzone and Burritos

Sophie Porter

In Southern California, ham sandwiches are made with burritos, the wheat flour tortillas, as often as they are made with the more familiar sliced white bread. In Northern California, sourdough bread is a staple, and many Californians insist that it's the same as, or far better than, French bread. If the breads have an added fillip of flavor, so do the pizzas—especially the calzone which includes local goat cheese among the ingredients. Garlic, ripe olives, Monterey Jack cheese—these and other products of California are often featured in their baked goods.

San Francisco's Sourdough Bread

Located in San Francisco's airport are bins of that city's favorite sourdough bread: "Take home a loaf of sourdough bread," a sign exhorts. But what happens after you've gotten home, and you want still more sourdough bread? For those lovers of sourdough, here's a recipe for this beloved California bread. It takes a bit of time because sourdough starter must be prepared first, and then allowed to ferment for anywhere from 2 to 10 days, depending on the warmth of the room where the starter is kept.

Sourdough Starter

1 envelope active dry yeast
2 cups warm water (110 degrees)
2 cups all-purpose flour

In a 6-cup glass, pottery, or plastic container, combine yeast, water, and flour, until mixture is smooth. Cover the container with cheesecloth or a dishcloth, and allow to stand at room temperature for at least 2 days, stirring 3 or 4 times.

Do not use a metal container because starter is acidic. Starter should be covered lightly while at room temperature because it is fermenting and might explode if sealed.

The starter is ready to use when it is bubbly and has a slightly sour smell. After spooning off the cup of starter needed for the following recipe, replenish the remainder of the starter by adding 1 cup of flour and 1 cup of warm water. Follow the same procedure until the new batch is bubbly. Transfer to a glass or plastic container, cover, and refrigerate. If not used within 10 days, add ½ teaspoon of sugar to the starter when you want to use it once again. This will start up the fermentation process.

If you refrigerate the starter in a tightly sealed container for longer than 10 days, open the container every 2 weeks to allow gases to escape, or store in a plastic container with a lid. Once again, never seal the starter container when you have it at room temperature.

Sourdough Bread

1½ cups warm water
1 cup Sourdough Starter
6 cups all-purpose flour
3 teaspoons sugar
1½ teaspoons salt
1 teaspoon baking soda

Combine warm water, starter, 4 cups of the flour, sugar, and salt in a large pottery or glass bowl. Mix thoroughly, cover with cheesecloth or a dish towel, and allow to stand at room temperature for 18 to 24 hours, or until dough has doubled.

Combine 1 cup of the remaining flour with ½ teaspoon of the baking soda and add to risen dough, working until dough is stiff.

Turn dough out onto a floured board, and knead in remaining cup of flour and ½ teaspoon baking soda. Knead for 5 to 10 minutes, or until dough is smooth.

Divide dough in half, and shape each half into a round or long loaf. Place loaves on a lightly greased baking sheet, cover with cheesecloth or a dish towel, and allow to stand in a warm place for approximately 3 to 4 hours, or until loaves have almost doubled in size.

Brush loaves lightly with water, and slash loaves with a sharp knife, making 3 or 4 diagonal cuts across the top of each loaf.

Bake in a preheated 400° oven for 50 to 60 minutes, or until crusts are golden brown.

For crustier loaves, place a shallow pan filled with water in the bottom of the oven.

Yield: 2 loaves

Olive Onion Bread

2 cups biscuit mix
2 tablespoons chopped parsley
⅔ cup cold water
2 cups thinly sliced onions
2 tablespoons butter
Salt and freshly ground black pepper to taste
½ cup sour cream
1 egg, beaten
1 teaspoon dried dillweed
¾ cup pitted ripe olives (black California olives), sliced

Combine biscuit mix, parsley, and cold water. Spoon into a greased 8 X 8 pan. Sauté onions in butter until golden, and season with salt and pepper.

Combine sour cream, egg, dillweed, and olives. Add onions and mix. Spoon over bread.

Bake in preheated 450° oven for 20 minutes. Cut into squares.

Serves: 6

Green Chili Spoon Bread

¾ cup yellow cornmeal
1½ cups cold water
4 tablespoons butter, softened
2 cups shredded Tillamook or Cheddar cheese
1 teaspoon salt
1 cup milk
4 egg yolks, beaten
1 can (4 ounces) green chili peppers, chopped
1 cup pitted ripe olives (black California olives), sliced
4 egg whites, beaten until stiff

Combine cornmeal and water in a saucepan, and cook, stirring constantly, until mixture comes to a boil and thickens. Remove from heat.

Add butter, cheese, and salt to cornmeal. Combine milk and egg yolks, and stir into cornmeal mixture. Add chili peppers and olives. Stir to combine.

Fold egg whites into cornmeal mixture, and pour into a large, cast iron frying pan or into an ovenproof casserole. Even out cornmeal mixture, and bake in preheated 325° oven for 50 to 60 minutes, or until spoon bread is brown and puffy. Test by inserting a knife blade into center of spoon bread. Blade should come out clean and dry when spoon bread is done.

Serve by spooning bread onto individual dishes.

Serves: 8

Vegetable Quiche in Garlic Crust

1 cup all-purpose flour
1¼ teaspoons salt
4 tablespoons vegetable shortening
4 tablespoons butter
1 small clove garlic, pressed
¾ cup milk, approximately
1 cup sliced mushrooms
2 cloves garlic, minced
1 cup chopped spinach
½ cup grated carrots
2 eggs
½ teaspoon chopped fresh dillweed
¾ cup grated Swiss cheese

To prepare garlic crust, combine flour and ½ teaspoon of salt, then cut in vegetable shortening and 2 tablespoons of the butter until mixture forms particles the size of peas. Add pressed garlic. Sprinkle 1½ tablespoons of the milk over the flour mixture and work into a dough, adding more milk if necessary. Shape into a ball, and refrigerate for 30 minutes. Garlic crust dough may also be prepared in a food processor.

Heat remaining 2 tablespoons of butter in a large skillet. Add mushrooms and garlic, and sauté, stirring, for 5 minutes. Add spinach. Cover skillet, and cook for 2 to 3 minutes, or until spinach is wilted. Remove from heat, stir in carrots, and reserve.

In a bowl, combine eggs, ⅔ cup of milk, ¾ teaspoon of salt, and dillweed and beat well. Stir in cheese, mixing well. Add vegetable mixture. Combine all ingredients thoroughly and reserve.

Roll garlic crust into a circle and fit into an 8-inch quiche pan that is ¾ inch deep. Place a sheet of foil on the crust, and add dry beans or aluminum pie-weights.

Partially bake crust in preheated 425° oven for 10 minutes. Remove foil and weights and allow crust to cool for 10 minutes.

Pour egg-vegetable mixture into garlic crust. Place quiche on the lowest rack of a preheated 350° oven and bake for 35 minutes, or until a sharp knife inserted close to the center of the filling comes out clean. Allow to cool for 15 minutes before serving.

Serves: 6–8

Olive and Chili Pie

1 cup milk
2 eggs
⅓ cup all-purpose flour
½ pound Monterey Jack cheese, grated
½ pound Cheddar cheese, grated
1 partially baked 9-inch pie shell
1 can (7 ounces) whole green chilies, chopped or cut in large pieces
1 cup pitted ripe olives (black California olives), halved
1 cup tomato sauce

Combine milk, eggs, and flour in a blender or food processor, and blend thoroughly.
Combine cheeses. Measure ½ cup of the mixed cheese and reserve. Spoon into pie shell half the remaining cheese. Combine chilies and olives, and spoon half of chili-olive mixture over grated cheese. Pour on half milk-egg mixture.
Repeat with cheese, chili-olive mixture, and milk-egg mixture. Spoon tomato sauce over all.
Bake pie in preheated 375° oven, for 45 minutes. Top with reserved grated cheese, and bake for an additional 5 to 10 minutes, or until a knife blade inserted close to the center of the filling comes out clean.

Serves: 4–6 as a main dish; 10–12 as an appetizer

Calzone from Café Chez Panisse

Alice Waters's Chez Panisse in Berkeley is divided into two floors and two attitudes. The restaurant downstairs serves California cuisine—recently re-labeled New American cuisine since its move east—while the more informal Café upstairs serves food with a decidedly Italian flavor. A favorite at the Café is the following very special calzone.

1 cup warm water
½ teaspoon sugar
1 envelope active dry yeast
3 cups sifted all-purpose flour
2 tablespoons vegetable oil
½ teaspoon salt
12 ounces mozzarella cheese, shredded
6 ounces creamy goat cheese, crumbled
3 ounces sliced prosciutto, cut into strips
3 tablespoons chopped chives
1 tablespoon finely minced garlic
1 tablespoon vegetable oil
6 teaspoons grated Parmesan cheese

Combine warm water and sugar in a mixing bowl, and sprinkle with yeast. Let stand 5 minutes to soften. Add half the flour, and knead until smooth. Stir in oil and salt. Gradually blend in remaining flour to make a moderately stiff dough. Turn out onto lightly floured board and knead smooth. Return dough to bowl, cover, and allow to rise in a warm place until doubled.

When dough has risen, punch down and divide into 3 pieces. Roll each piece on a lightly floured board into a 9-inch circle. Place a third of the mozzarella, goat cheese, and prosciutto on each circle of dough. Combine chives and garlic, and sprinkle over filling. Moisten edges, and fold over to enclose filling, pressing edges firmly together.

Place on lightly greased baking sheets. Let rise until dough feels light to the touch, about 30 to 45 minutes.

Bake in center of a preheated 375° oven for 30 to 35 minutes, or until browned. Remove from oven and brush top crust with oil. Sprinkle with grated Parmesan cheese. Serve warm.

Yield: 3 large calzone

Quick California Takes

Burritos (wheat flour tortillas), rather than bread, are often used in southern California as an interesting sandwich base.

To make a burrito sandwich: place ½ cup of guacamole, or chicken salad, or tuna salad in the center of a warmed burrito. Fold in the ends, and then roll from one side to the other.

A combination of ham, cheese, and shredded lettuce on a burrito also makes life more interesting. Add a bit of your favorite Salsa Mexicana to this one (p. 134).

Burritos (Wheat Flour Tortillas)

Wheat flour tortillas, or burritos, are readily available in California markets, but have not yet made their way completely across the country; hence the following recipe for homemade burritos.

4 cups all-purpose flour
2 teaspoons salt
½ cup vegetable shortening
1 cup lukewarm water

Combine flour with salt. Cut in shortening and add lukewarm water gradually. Dough should be stiff.

Place dough on a floured board and knead thoroughly. Divide dough into 12 pieces, and roll each piece into a ball. Cover dough balls with a damp cloth and let rest for 15 minutes.

Roll out each ball into an approximately 8-inch circle. Cook on a medium-hot, ungreased skillet or griddle, turning once. Burritos should have golden brown spots, but should not be brown all over.

Yield: 12

Special 10 Touches: Sauces, Relishes and Butters

Sophie Porter

Plain and simple is just not Californian. A sauce or a special butter adds an interesting note to many dishes. A sauceboat might hold a fiery concoction reminiscent of Mexico, while at other times the offering is pure California, melding grapes, wine, and white grape juice in an original creation. Chutney becomes more interesting and less familiar when it's prepared with California-grown figs.

Barbecue Sauce St. Helena

1 cup vegetable oil
1 tablespoon chopped parsley
2 tablespoons catsup
1 teaspoon Dijon mustard
1 teaspoon Worcestershire sauce
1 clove Elephant Garlic, mashed (or 1 clove garlic, pressed)
Salt and freshly ground black pepper to taste

Place all ingredients in a food processor or blender and blend until smooth.
Use to baste meats, poultry, or fish while barbecuing.

Yield: 1½ cups, approximately

Golden Caviar Sauce

½ cup sour cream
½ cup heavy sweet cream (whipping cream)
¼ cup minced green onion or scallions
4 ounces Golden Caviar

Place sour cream, sweet cream, and onion in a bowl and mix thoroughly. Add caviar and stir very gently.
Use as a dip for fresh vegetables, or spoon over cooked thin pasta, such as angel hair pasta, or fettucine. The sauce may also be used as a garnish for sautéed scallops or fish fillets.

Yield: 1½ cups, approximately

Quick California Takes

Flavored Butters to Add a Fillip to Fish, Meat or Vegetables:

Combine 3 tablespoons softened butter with 1 tablespoon sun-dried tomatoes or 1 tablespoon tomato purée. Mix thoroughly. Excellent over cooked string beans or broiled fish fillets.

Combine 2 tablespoons softened butter with ¼ to ½ teaspoon curry powder. Mix thoroughly. Use as a garnish for broiled shrimp or broiled breast of chicken.

Combine 4 tablespoons softened butter with 1 teaspoon freshly grated horseradish. Mix thoroughly. Spoon over boiled new potatoes or grilled halibut fillets.

Combine 3 tablespoons softened butter with 2 finely chopped walnuts. Mix thoroughly. Use as a garnish for broiled, thinly sliced steak or cooked fettucine.

Hot Garlic-Anchovy Sauce

3 cloves Elephant Garlic, minced, or 1 clove garlic, pressed
½ cup olive oil
8 anchovy fillets, chopped
1 cup butter

Sauté garlic in olive oil until soft. Do not brown; this causes garlic to lose its flavor.

Remove pan from heat and add anchovies. Crush with wooden spoon against side of frying pan, then mix well with garlic. Add butter and heat thoroughly. Transfer mixture to a chafing dish.

Serve as a dip for raw cauliflower, broccoli, celery, and mushrooms.

Yield: 1½ cups, approximately

Grape and Leek Sauce with Wine

The news here is the use of white grape juice and whole fresh grapes in combination with dry white wine. The result is a sauce that is both naturally sweet and piquant. Grape and Leek Sauce can turn a simple roast chicken into a party dish, and it's a marvelous accompaniment to roast quail, ducks, and game hens.

4 leeks, white part only
6 tablespoons butter
1½ cups chicken broth
2½ cups white grape juice
2 cups dry white wine
Small bunch of seedless grapes, red Emperor or white
2 tablespoons cornstarch

Clean leeks thoroughly. Slice white part of leeks into thin pieces. Melt 4 tablespoons of the butter in a large saucepan and add leeks. Sauté for 3 or 4 minutes, stirring occasionally. Add chicken broth, cover, and simmer until leeks are barely tender.

Add 2 cups of the grape juice and all the wine to leeks and cook, uncovered, for 20 minutes. Sauce will reduce and alcoholic intensity of the wine will diminish. Add remaining 2 tablespoons of butter, and stir until melted. Add grapes. Reserve.

Combine cornstarch and remaining ½ cup grape juice; stir to dissolve. Off heat, stir cornstarch mixture into sauce. Return to heat, and simmer for 5 to 10 minutes until sauce thickens slightly.

Yield: 5 cups, approximately

Green Salsa Mexicana I

3 tablespoons pepitas (toasted, salted pumpkin seeds)
1 can (4 ounces) green chili peppers
8 sprigs parsley
2 cups chicken broth
Salt and freshly ground black pepper to taste

Combine all ingredients in a food processor or blender and purée thoroughly. Heat before serving.

Yield: 2½ cups, approximately

Salsa Mexicana II

1 clove garlic, minced
1 tablespoon vegetable oil
1 cup tomato sauce
1 large tomato, peeled and chopped
⅓ cup water
¼ cup chopped onion
1–2 tablespoons chopped fresh coriander, or *cilantro* (optional)
Grated peel and juice of ½ lemon
¼ teaspoon salt
1 or 2 small, fresh serrano or jalapeño chili peppers, or ½–1 teaspoon red pepper flakes, or ½ cup chopped, canned green chili
   peppers

In a small saucepan, sauté garlic in oil until tender. Remove from heat and stir in remaining ingredients. Mix thoroughly. Allow flavors to blend for 1 hour before serving.

Yield: 2 cups, approximately

Salsa Mexicana III

1 large onion, chopped
1 pound tomatoes, peeled and chopped fine
3 serrano chili peppers, chopped
2 sprigs fresh coriander (*cilantro*), chopped, use parsley if coriander
   is not available, but the flavor won't be the same
1 clove garlic, chopped
1 teaspoon salt

Combine all ingredients, and allow flavors to blend for 1 hour before serving.

Yield: 2 cups, approximately

Sauce Louis

Tourists and natives alike walk around San Francisco's Fisherman's Wharf eating out of paper cups filled with cold crabmeat topped with a spicy sauce. This eat-as-you-walk dish is called Crab Louis, pronounced "Looey," and here is Sauce Louis which goes as well with cold shrimp as it does with crabmeat.

1½ cups mayonnaise
¼ cup heavy sweet cream (whipping cream)
¼ cup chili sauce
4 green onions, or scallions, finely chopped
2 teaspoons lemon juice
Salt and freshly ground black pepper to taste

Place all ingredients in a bowl and mix thoroughly. Refrigerate for at least 2 hours before using to allow flavors to blend.

Yield: 2 cups, approximately

Plum Sauce for Roast Pork or Lamb

1 pound red plums
2 teaspoons lemon juice
¼ teaspoon ground ginger
¼ teaspoon ground cardamom
½ teaspoon hot pepper sauce
2 tablespoons sugar

Remove pits from plums. Using a food processor or blender, purée plums.
Combine plum purée and all other ingredients in a saucepan. Mix thoroughly. Cook over low heat until mixture has thickened. Add more hot pepper sauce or sugar, if desired.
Use hot or cold as an accompaniment with pork or lamb, and as a final basting ingredient for roast pork.

Yield: 2 cups, approximately

Kiwi-Grape Sauce

¼ cup sugar
4½ teaspoons cornstarch
½ teaspoon salt
¾ cup water
3 tablespoons dry white wine
2 tablespoons cider vinegar
2 teaspoons soy sauce
1 teaspoon slivered fresh ginger
1 medium kiwi fruit, peeled and thinly sliced
1 cup halved red grapes, seeded if necessary

In a small bowl, combine sugar, cornstarch, and salt. Combine water, wine, vinegar, soy sauce, and ginger in a saucepan. Add cornstarch mixture and cook, stirring until sauce has thickened and is clear.

Add kiwi fruit and grapes and heat thoroughly. Serve with poultry, pork, or fish.

Yield: 2 cups, approximately

Jim's Skordalia Sauce or Spread

Serve this with crackers or as a sauce with roast leg of lamb, broiled fish, or broiled chicken.

2 large potatoes, peeled, cooked, and mashed
3 cloves Elephant Garlic (or 2 cloves garlic) peeled
2 tablespoons Dijon mustard
1 tablespoon white vinegar
1 teaspoon Worcestershire sauce
1 cup vegetable oil
Salt and freshly ground pepper to taste
2 cups mayonnaise
4 green onions, or scallions, finely chopped

Combine all ingredients except scallions in a food processor or electric mixer. Process until you have a smooth purée. If you're using a food processor, pulse, or turn machine on and off, and be careful not to overprocess, or potatoes will have a pasty consistency.

Spoon purée into a serving bowl and garnish with chopped green onions.

Yield: 5 cups, approximately

Quick California Takes

With Papaya:

Baked Papaya

Cut a papaya in half, seed and peel. Place papaya on a shallow broiler tray. Dot with butter and sprinkle brown sugar and cinnamon on each half. Broil until butter has melted and brown sugar bubbles. Serve with baked ham or roast pork.

Teatime Spread

Peel, seed, and slice papaya. Place fruit in food processor or blender. Add 1 cup plain yogurt, and process only until ingredients are combined. Serve over a wedge of cream cheese with toast or sesame seed crackers.

Fig Chutney

2 cups chopped dried figs (about 28 figs)
2 apples, peeled and chopped
1 medium onion, finely chopped
1 lemon, sliced paper thin
1 cup seedless raisins
¾ cup dark brown sugar, firmly packed
½ cup molasses
1 cup white vinegar
½ teaspoon ground cloves
1 teaspoon ground ginger
½ teaspoon ground cinnamon

In a large, heavy saucepan, mix all ingredients thoroughly. Bring to a boil, stirring frequently. Reduce heat and simmer, uncovered, stirring occasionally for about 1 hour, or until dark and thick. Pack into sterilized ½-pint or 1-pint canning jars and seal at once.

Yield: 2 pints, approximately

California Pickled Figs

If you're looking for a different and delicious relish to accompany roast meat or chicken, serve these pickled figs.

1½ cups dried figs (12 ounces)
1½ cups water
1 cup white vinegar
1½ cups light brown sugar, firmly packed
2 pieces cinnamon stick
1 teaspoon whole cloves
1 teaspoon ground allspice

Pierce figs with a sharp fork. Reserve.

Combine water, vinegar, sugar, and spices in saucepan. Bring to boil. Add figs, cover, and simmer for 35 minutes.

Cool figs in liquid. Refrigerate until ready to serve. Store in refrigerator.

Yield: 3½ cups

Napa Valley Relish

3 medium zucchini, coarsely shredded
2 stalks celery, sliced thin
½ green bell pepper, seeded and coarsely shredded
1 small yellow onion, chopped
1 clove Elephant Garlic, minced (or 1 clove garlic, pressed)
⅔ cup cider vinegar
2 tablespoons white wine vinegar
⅓ cup vegetable oil
½ cup sugar
1 teaspoon salt
¼ teaspoon freshly ground black pepper
¼ cup dry white wine

Place all ingredients in a large bowl. Mix thoroughly.

Cover and refrigerate for 4 to 6 hours before serving.

Will keep in refrigerator for 2 weeks.

Yield: 3–4 cups, approximately

Apple-Plum Butter

2 pounds red plums, quartered
2 pounds apples, peeled, cored and quartered
2 cups water
2¾ cups sugar
2 teaspoons ground cinnamon
1 teaspoon grated nutmeg
¼ teaspoon ground allspice

Combine plums, apples, and water in a heavy saucepan. Bring mixture to a boil. Reduce heat and cook until fruit is very tender.

Remove from heat and purée in a food processor or blender. Return fruit purée to saucepan and add remaining ingredients. Cook over low heat until butter is thick and glossy.

Yield: 3 pints

Prune Butter

4 cups pitted prunes
2 cups orange juice
¼ cup dark brown sugar, firmly packed
½ cup water
1 teaspoon grated lemon peel

Combine prunes, orange juice, sugar, and water in a saucepan. Bring to a boil. Reduce heat and simmer for 10 minutes, stirring from time to time. Remove from heat and allow to cool for 10 minutes.

Using a food processor or blender, process prunes and cooking liquid until thoroughly puréed.

Return prune purée to saucepan. Add lemon peel and cook, stirring, for 5 to 10 minutes, or until mixture has the consistency of jam.

Yield: 2 pints, approximately

Desserts 11 in Abundance: Light or Rich

Sophie Porter

Desserts run the gamut of sweet experiences in California. Some days (even the most hedonistic does feel an occasional puritanical twinge) dessert may be no more than a blushing peach or a tender apricot. But then, as days go by, fresh fruits are transmuted into fruit sorbets, and still later, shimmering cold mousses, cream-laden tarts, and chocolate excesses are brought to the table. A variety of desserts may be part of the entertainment when guests are invited to a dessert and wine party, and only the most disciplined can resist the rich offerings bountifully displayed.

Cantaloupe Sorbet

1 very ripe cantaloupe
1½ cups sugar
⅓ cup water
Juice of 1 lemon

Cut cantaloupe in half. Clean out seeds and scoop out melon pulp. Place pulp in a food processor or blender, and purée. You should have 2 cups of melon purée.

Combine sugar and water in a saucepan and bring to a boil. Cook for 2 minutes, stirring from time to time. Allow to cool for 10 minutes.

Combine melon purée and syrup and stir thoroughly. Stir in lemon juice, mixing well.

Pour melon mixture into container of an ice cream maker and, following manufacturer's directions, process until frozen.

Serves: 6

California Champagne Sorbet

1¼ cups sugar
1¼ cups water
Juice of 3 lemons (about ½ cup)
1 cup California Champagne
2 egg whites

Combine 1 cup of the sugar with water in a saucepan. Cook, stirring, until mixture comes to a boil and sugar is dissolved. Remove from heat, add lemon juice, and stir in Champagne. Cover and refrigerate until chilled.

Combine remaining ¼ cup of sugar with 2 tablespoons of water in a saucepan. Cook, stirring, until mixture comes to a boil and sugar is dissolved. Remove from heat.

Beat egg whites until foamy, then gradually beat in sugar syrup. Beat until egg whites are stiff.

Stir Champagne mixture into egg whites. Do not blend. Pour Champagne-egg white mixture into container of an ice cream maker and, following manufacturer's directions, process until frozen.

Serves: 6

Fresh Fruit Sorbet

The perfect light ending to dinner is a fruit sorbet. The following recipe can be used for peaches, apricots, or plums—the fruit must be ripe and beautifully unblemished.

2½   pounds of peaches, apricots, or plums
1½   cups sugar
⅔   cup water
Juice of 2 lemons

Place fruit of your choice in a large saucepan filled with boiling water. Cook for approximately 5 minutes, or until fruit can be easily peeled.

Allow fruit to cool sufficiently to handle, and then peel and pit fruit. Using a food processor, blender, or food mill, purée the fruit. You should have 2 cups of purée. Reserve fruit purée.

Combine sugar and water in a saucepan. Cook, stirring, until mixture comes to a boil. Boil for 2 minutes. Allow syrup to cool for 15 minutes. Do not refrigerate, as chilling will harden syrup.

Combine purée and syrup, mixing thoroughly. Stir in lemon juice. Pour fruit mixture into container of an ice cream maker and, following manufacturer's directions, process until frozen.

Serves: 6

Lemon Granita

4 cups water
1 cup sugar
1 tablespoon grated fresh lemon peel
⅔ cup lemon juice
Dash of salt

In a saucepan, combine water and sugar. Bring to a boil, stirring to dissolve sugar. Add lemon peel, juice, and salt. Pour into 13×9×2-inch baking pan. Freeze until icy, about 3 hours, stirring occasionally.

Serves: 6

Fresh Raspberry Sorbet

2–2½ pounds ripe raspberries
Juice of 1 lemon, strained
Juice of 1 orange, strained
1½ cups sugar

Using a blender, food processor, or food mill, purée raspberries thoroughly. You should have 2 cups of purée. If you have used a food mill and fruit is not thoroughly puréed, press through a fine strainer.

Combine lemon juice, orange juice, and sugar in a saucepan. Heat over very low heat, stirring constantly, and cook only until sugar has melted. Remove from heat at once. Allow to cool for 10 minutes.

Combine raspberry purée with lemon juice mixture, stirring until thoroughly blended.

Pour raspberry mixture into container of an ice cream maker and, following manufacturer's directions, process until frozen.

Serves: 6

Apricot Yogurt Dessert

4 cups sliced fresh apricots
2 cups yogurt
2 tablespoons sugar
½ teaspoon grated lemon peel
2 apricots, sliced

Place sliced apricots in each of 8 sherbert glasses. Combine yogurt, sugar and lemon peel; spoon over apricots. Garnish with apricot slices.

Serves: 8

Peach Clafouti

A clafouti is first cousin to a soufflé and a close relative of the custard, but it is easier to prepare than either of those dishes. In France it is traditionally made with fresh cherries. Californians, however, have translated this recipe and made it part of the new American cuisine by using peaches. It tastes every bit as good, and it's much easier to pit a peach than a cherry. Clafouti can also be made with grapes or plums.

¾ cup milk
½ teaspoon almond extract
2 tablespoons sugar
2 eggs
3 tablespoons all-purpose flour
1 tablespoon butter, melted
2 medium peaches, pitted and cut into 6 wedges each
Powdered sugar

Place milk, almond extract, sugar, eggs, flour, and melted butter in a food processor or blender, and blend thoroughly. Arrange peach wedges in a buttered, shallow, 3-cup baking dish.

Pour milk mixture over peaches. Bake in a preheated 350° preheated oven for 40 to 45 minutes, or until clafouti is puffed and brown. Sprinkle powdered sugar over clafouti and serve immediately.

Serves: 4

Grape Clafouti

1½ pounds seedless grapes
1½ cups milk
4 eggs
2 teaspoons vanilla extract
½ cup all-purpose flour
½ cup sugar
Powdered sugar

Cut grapes in half, and place on bottom of a buttered two-quart baking dish.

Combine milk and all other ingredients in a food processor, or blender, and blend thoroughly. Pour milk mixture over the grapes.

Bake in a preheated 350° oven for approximately 1 hour, or until clafouti is puffed and brown. A sharp knife piercing the center should come out clean.

Sprinkle with powdered sugar and serve immediately.

Serves: 4–6

Jim Nassikas and the Stanford Court Hotel of Nob Hill

When talking to Californians about the latest and best in food and wine, the question is frequently asked, "Do you know Jim Nassikas?"

Jim Nassikas is the creator and president of San Francisco's Stanford Court Hotel which features many aspects of the good life: excellent service, luxurious atmosphere, fine food, and the wine to go with it.

Jim Nassikas says that the hotel is his dream come true; it is also the dream come true of many of the guests who stay there. They enjoy the Nassikas version of what a fine hotel should offer: personal, caring service, beautiful furnishings—wooden armoires, marble-topped tables and floors, exquisite crystal chandeliers, antiques—and never a glimpse of formica or plastic.

The Stanford Court believes in pampering; there are heated towel racks in the bathrooms and extra television sets in the dressing rooms. The discreet phone booth near the restaurant has wallpaper that matches the upholstery on the French period chair.

It's all part of Nassikas's philosophy acquired at the Swiss Hotel School in Lausanne. "The Swiss taught me quality...to value the human scale ... and that the individual counts most."

Because it is the individual that counts most—a true California concept, though Nassikas was born in New Hampshire—there is never a convention at the Stanford Court. Guests are paged by a green-uniformed bellman carrying a blackboard aloft with the guest's name written on it. Messages are tucked into tiny envelopes, and hotel operators call to make sure that messages are received.

Elegance continues in Fournou's Bar, built to resemble an art-nouveau conservatory, and in the Café Potpourri, but it is in Fournou's Ovens, the hotel's restaurant, where Jim Nassikas's ideas are most evident. From the very beginning, he was determined that the restaurant would be as fine as an excellent independent restaurant. It would be "scaled to fit people" and it would have "a wide range of monumentally magnificent trivialities."

Possibly trivial, but certainly beautiful, are the antique armoires, chests, wall brackets, and paintings that decorate the restaurant. Decorative, but far from trivial, are the huge, working ovens faced in French Provincial tile.

The menu combines the classic with the Californian. Rack of lamb with sauce aux aromates is roasted over an oakwood fire in the oven; chicken flavored with tarragon is called roast Sonoma chicken a l'estragon; artichokes—one of California's signature crops—appear in an exquisite cream of artichoke soup with hazelnuts.

The newest and best of California foods and wines are offered at Fournou's Ovens. Golden Caviar was first featured there, and is served as an appetizer stuffed lavishly into tiny, new potatoes. Jim Nassikas has concentrated on California wines, and is aware of those offered by the smallest wineries. Regular customers have their own private wine bins, with their names etched on elegant plaques, in the hotel's wine cellers.

The Stanford Court is deservedly successful, which means that the hotel president could take off a few days now and again. But not Jim Nassikas. He's right there at his dream hotel, checking the quality of the lamb and the lettuce at the restaurant, tasting a new Chenin Blanc from a hitherto unknown winery, looking quickly into the Café Potpourri—are the plants fresh and green?—and stopping to talk to a guest, asking—as though it really mattered, and to this man it does—if everything is all right, if the service is as expected, and if there is anything more that might be done.

Many guests tell Jim Nassikas that they don't want to leave his hotel. Not ever. He's happy to hear that, and credits the compliment to his seemingly unreasonable demand for perfection. He explained that George Bernard Shaw said, "All progress depends on the unreasonable man," and Jim Nassikas is a very unreasonable man.

Cold Lemon Mousse in the Style of Fournou's Ovens

6 eggs, separated
14 tablespoons sugar
⅓ cup dry white wine
1 envelope unflavored gelatin
¾ cup freshly squeezed lemon juice
1 teaspoon grated lemon peel
1 pint heavy sweet cream (whipping cream), whipped

Beat egg yolks until thick and lemon colored. Reserve.
Combine 8 tablespoons of the sugar with the wine and cook, stirring, until sugar is dissolved and a thick syrup forms.

Soften gelatin in 2 tablespoons of water and stir into the syrup. Stir in lemon juice and peel. Add egg yolks and stir until mixture is thick and thoroughly combined.

Fold whipped cream into egg yolk mixture.

Beat egg whites until soft peaks are reached and then gradually add the remaining 6 tablespoons of sugar and beat until whites have formed stiff peaks.

Fold egg whites into whipped cream-egg yolk mixture.

Spoon mousse into a 9-inch soufflé dish or into individual dessert or mousse dishes. Refrigerate for at least 4 hours. (Dessert may be prepared on day before serving.)

Serves: 8

Frozen Peach Mousse

2½ pounds peaches (about 8)
4 eggs, separated
¾ cup sugar
¼ cup lemon juice
4 tablespoons peach liqueur (optional)

Peel and slice about 1–1½ pounds of the peaches. Place sliced peaches in food processor or blender, or use a food mill, and purée peaches. You should have 1 cup. Refrigerate purée.

In the top of a double boiler, beat egg yolks with ½ cup of sugar until thick and lemony in color. Stir in the lemon juice and the peach liqueur, if you wish. Cook over hot water, stirring constantly, until mixture has thickened, about 4 minutes. Cool to room temperature and fold in peach purée. Chill in refrigerator.

In a mixing bowl, beat egg whites until foamy. Gradually add remaining ¼ cup of sugar, beating until meringue is stiff. Fold into peach mixture.

Spoon peach mousse into 8 custard cups and freeze. Before serving, peel and slice remaining peaches. To serve, unmold frozen mousse onto individual dessert plates and garnish with sliced peaches. Mousse tastes best if allowed to stand and soften 5 to 10 minutes before serving.

Serves: 8

Light Raspberry Soufflé

Raymond Dreyfus, the Chef de Cuisine of the L'Escoffier Restaurant in Beverly Hills, has created a raspberry soufflé that is so light it's positively ethereal. He uses no flour or milk-based sauce to distract from the luscious flavor of the fresh raspberries.

1 cup heavy cream (whipping cream)
¼ cup grenadine syrup
½ pound fresh raspberries, puréed
¾ cup sugar
4 egg whites
2 tablespoons butter, melted

Whip cream until thick. Add grenadine to cream, and continue whipping until firm peaks form. Refrigerate whipped cream.

Combine raspberry purée with 3 tablespoons of the sugar. Mix thoroughly.

Beat egg whites with remaining sugar until stiff. Fold raspberry purée into egg whites.

Prepare 6 individual ramekins or soufflé dishes by coating with melted butter and dusting with sugar. Fill ramekins with the egg and raspberry mixture. Bake on the upper level of a preheated 350° oven for 8 to 10 minutes, or until the soufflés rise about halfway above the rims of the ramekins.

Top soufflés with prepared whipped cream.

Serves: 6

Wine-Grape Dessert

1 envelope unflavored gelatin
½ cup apple juice
¼ cup sugar
1½ cups semi-dry white wine
1½ cups halved green grapes, seeded if necessary
1 cup diced red apples
½ cup sliced almonds, toasted

Soften gelatin in apple juice; heat to dissolve. Add sugar and cook until sugar has dissolved. Stir in wine and chill until slightly firm.

Stir in grapes, apples, and almonds. Spoon into stemmed goblets or sherbet dishes, and chill until firm.

Serves: 6

Macaroon Cream

¾ cup sugar
¼ cup water
4 egg yolks
18 macaroons
¼ cup Amaretto or other almond-flavored liqueur
1½ cups heavy sweet cream (whipping cream), whipped
Strawberries (optional)

Combine sugar and water in a saucepan and bring to a boil. Cook until mixture reaches the soft ball stage.

Beat egg yolks until thick and lemon colored. Gradually add sugar syrup to egg yolks, stirring constantly. Beat sugar-egg mixture until all ingredients are combined, and mixture is fluffy and thick. Refrigerate until thoroughly chilled.

Dip macaroons into liqueur, and stand up around the inside edge of a 9-inch springform pan.

Fold whipped cream into egg yolks mixture and spoon into springform pan. Cover with foil and freeze until firm.

Before serving, place pan on a serving platter and remove sides. Serve with sliced strawberries, if you wish.

Serves: 6–8

Chocolate Dipped Fruits

Strawberries, orange slices, and grapes dipped into chocolate, the perfect dessert to offer with espresso coffee at the end of a meal. Remember that fruits, especially strawberries, tend to "weep," so prepare and serve this dessert on a cool day.

1 quart strawberries, unhulled
2 mandarin, tangerine, or navel oranges, peeled and sectioned
1 pound seedless grapes
1 pound semisweet chocolate

Melt chocolate in top of a double boiler, stirring until thoroughly melted and smooth.

Holding strawberries by the stems, dip each one halfway into melted chocolate. Repeat with orange sections, and with grapes.

Place chocolate-dipped fruits on a flat platter and refrigerate until chocolate hardens.

Serves: 15, approximately

Baked Fig Pudding and Sauce

12 Calimyrna dried figs
1 cup all-purpose flour
½ cup granulated sugar
2 teaspoons baking powder
¼ teaspoon salt
½ cup chopped nuts (almonds or walnuts)
½ cup milk
2 tablespoons vegetable oil
1 teaspoon vanilla extract
¾ cup light brown sugar, firmly packed
1½ cups boiling water
1 tablespoon butter

Cut stems from figs and discard. Chop figs coarsely to make 1 cup. Set aside.

Combine flour, sugar, baking powder, and salt in a mixing bowl and mix well. Stir in figs and nuts. Stir in milk, oil and vanilla. Mix thoroughly. Spoon batter into a greased, 8-inch square pan.

Combine sugar, boiling water, and butter. Stir until sugar is dissolved and butter is melted. Carefully pour over unbaked batter. Bake in a 350° oven for 40 minutes, or until the batter rises to the top of pan. There will be sauce on top. Serve pudding and sauce warm.

Serves: 6

Sugared Grape Clusters

Beautiful as a garnish, perfect as a simple dessert, are clusters of grapes dipped into beaten egg white and rolled in sugar. This dish is most attractive when the grapes used are either red or black seedless grapes.

1 pound seedless grapes (red or black)
1 egg white, beaten
½ cup sugar

Cut grapes into individual serving-size clusters. Dip clusters into beaten egg white, then roll in sugar.

Place grapes on a flat platter or a board covered with waxed paper and allow to dry. Use as a garnish or serve as a dessert.

Serves: 6

Oranges in Red Wine

¾ cup sugar
1 cup water
1 cup dry red wine
1-inch piece stick cinnamon
1-inch piece vanilla bean
1 lemon, thinly sliced
6 large oranges, peeled and sliced thin

Combine sugar with water in a saucepan and cook, stirring, until the sugar dissolves.

Add wine, cinnamon, vanilla bean, and lemon and simmer for 20 minutes.

Pour the hot wine syrup over the oranges, cool to room temperature, and refrigerate for 6 to 8 hours, or until chilled.

Serves: 6

Caramelized Mandarin Oranges

Many cuisines offer recipes for oranges in a carmelized syrup, but Californians, who borrow freely and happily from the many people who have come from other countries to settle in their state, use a Chinese spice blend when preparing this light dessert. In California this dessert is prepared with mandarin or temple oranges, or with tangelos, a cross between an orange and a grapefruit. If none of these oranges is available, any eating orange, preferably navel, will do almost as well.

6 mandarin oranges (or other eating oranges)
1¼ cups sugar
1 cup water
4 tablespoons Grand Marnier or Cointreau liqueur
1 teaspoon Chinese Five Spices Powder

Peel the oranges and reserve. Discard peel from 3 oranges, and retain peel from remaining 3 oranges. Scrape the white pulp from the orange peel, and cut the peel into julienne strips.

Place strips of peel in a saucepan, cover with water, and bring to a boil. Cook for 10 minutes. Drain peel and reserve.

Combine sugar and water in a saucepan, bring to a boil, and cook for 10 minutes, stirring from time to time. Mixture will be a thin syrup.

Off heat, and using a slotted spoon, place oranges in syrup one at a time, making sure oranges are saturated with the syrup.

Remove oranges and place on a rack with a plate underneath to catch dripping syrup.

Add orange peel, liqueur, and five spices powder to syrup. Cook over low heat until peel becomes transparent.

Place oranges on a serving platter and pour syrup and peel over them. Chill for 2 to 3 hours before serving.

Serves: 6

Pears Caramel

4 firm pears, peeled, cored, and quartered
8 tablespoons sugar
8 tablespoons butter
1 cup heavy sweet cream (whipping cream)

Place pear quarters in a shallow baking dish. Sprinkle with sugar, and dot with butter.

Bake in a preheated 500° oven for 15 or 20 minutes, or until sugar is dark brown and bubbling. Baste pears with sugar and pear juices once or twice.

When sugar is caramelized, remove pan from oven and pour cream over pears. Serve at once, spooning caramel cream over pears.

Serves: 4

Stuffed Pears in Red Wine

6 large ripe pears
6 tablespoons farmer cheese
2 tablespoons sugar
2 tablespoons light cream, approximately
6 walnuts, finely chopped
3 cups dry red wine
1 cup sugar
1-inch piece vanilla bean
5 or 6 whole black peppercorns

Peel the pears and core them from the bottom just far enough to get out the seeds and woody core.

Combine farmer cheese, sugar, and cream and mash, adding cream if necessary to produce the texture of creamy cream cheese. Mash in the walnuts and press this mixture into the pears.

In a large saucepan, combine the wine, sugar, vanilla bean, and peppercorns. Bring the mixture to a boil, making sure the sugar is dissolved, and add the pears. If the mixture does not cover the pears, add some water. Simmer the pears slowly until they are tender. Serve pears chilled in their syrup.

Serves: 6

Fresh Persimmon and Fig Dessert

When available in the fall, ripe persimmons and fresh figs combine to create an exotic, delicious, and simple dessert.

4 large very ripe persimmons
8 fresh ripe figs

Cut stems from persimmons, and cut each persimmon into quarters. Cut each fig into halves.

Alternate persimmon quarters with fig halves on 4 individual dessert plates.

Serves: 4

Hot Prune Puffs

2 cups pitted prunes (approximately 35 prunes)
1 cup orange juice
¼ cup powdered sugar
¼ teaspoon ground cinnamon
¾ cup all-purpose flour
¾ cup water
¼ cup cornstarch
1 egg white, beaten until stiff
Vegetable oil for deep frying

Combine prunes and orange juice, and allow prunes to macerate in juice for 4 hours, stirring from time to time.

Combine sugar and cinnamon. Mix thoroughly and reserve.

Combine flour and cornstarch with ¾ cup of water and mix until thoroughly blended. Fold in egg white.

Remove prunes from juice and dip, one at a time, in the batter. Make sure each prune is well coated.

Heat 3 inches of oil in a deep skillet or large saucepan and deep fry prune puffs until crisp and light brown. Drain on paper towels, sprinkle with cinnamon-sugar, and serve at once.

Serves: 8–10

Quick California Takes

Date Shake

Combine 1 cup of milk with 1 cup of pitted dates in a food processor or blender. Process until dates are coarsely chopped.

Add 1 pint of vanilla ice cream and process until thick and thoroughly blended.

Serves: 2–4

Lawry's California Center

In Los Angeles, just a mile from Dodger Stadium, there exists a 12½-acre garden oasis. Walk through a wrought iron gate, and beyond the adobe walls you'll find a setting reminiscent of the haciendas of old Mexico. If you wish, you may just stroll about admiring the Chinese fringe trees and the scarlet Olé roses, dipping your fingers in splashing fountains; or, if you prefer, take a table on a patio and sip chilled margaritas while nibbling on nachos and guacamole.

If you're hungrier than that, choose a restaurant—there are a number of them—and enjoy a Mexican lunch or dinner prepared with California flavor. The mariachi musicians will be happy to play your favorite Mexican songs.

After you eat, visit the Wine and Gourmet Shop, or take a look at the apple dolls and cactus plants at the gift shop. The prices at the shops, and at the restaurants, are comfortably low. This dream-like garden complex is a creation of Lawry Foods, Inc., and is their imaginative way of introducing the idea of Mexican-Californian food to the consumer.

But Lawry's goes many steps further, and the center also features Wine Festivals, Asian Feasts, and a California Harvest Fair complete with square dancing and a barbeque.

Want to learn how to braid garlic, or arrange flowers? There's a class given at Lawry's. And if you've long been admired for your jack o'lanterns, be sure to enter the Pumpkin Carving Contest at the Fiesta Dinner given on Halloween night.

Tortilla Flats as Served at Lawry's California Center

The chefs at Lawry's California Center in Los Angeles use burritos, wheat flour tortillas, in this dessert. It's a purely California creation, though it is based on a tortilla. Cornmeal tortillas cannot be substituted because, unlike wheat flour tortillas, they do not take on the texture of pastry when fried. If wheat flour tortillas are not available in your area, you can make your own (see page 130).

2 tablespoons sugar
1 teaspoon ground cinnamon
1 burrito (wheat flour tortilla)
Vegetable oil for frying
1 tablespoon melted butter
1 scoop vanilla ice cream
Sliced strawberries or sliced peaches
1 tablespoon toasted slivered almonds

Combine sugar and cinnamon and reserve.

Heat oil in a skillet and fry burrito on both sides until golden brown and puffy. Drain on a paper towel.

Brush burrito with melted butter, and sprinkle with cinnamon sugar. Top with ice cream and garnish with fruit and nuts.

Serves: 1

Baked Praline Ice Cream Pie with Rum Sauce

½ cup dark brown sugar, firmly packed
½ cup heavy sweet cream (whipping cream)
2 tablespoons butter
1 cup chopped pecans
1½ teaspoons vanilla extract
1½ quarts vanilla ice cream
1 baked 9-inch pastry shell
3 egg whites
¼ teaspoon cream of tartar
⅓ cup granulated sugar

Rum Sauce

2 egg yolks, beaten
½ teaspoon grated lemon peel
¼ cup lemon juice
⅓ cup sugar
4 tablespoons butter
3 tablespoons light rum

To prepare praline mixture:
In a saucepan, heat and stir brown sugar over medium-low heat until sugar melts, about 10 to 12 minutes. Add cream gradually. Cook 2 to 3 minutes more, or until smooth. Remove from heat and stir in butter, pecans, and 1 teaspoon of the vanilla. Remove from heat and allow to cool.

Stir ice cream just to soften; quickly fold in praline mixture. Spoon into pastry shell and place in freezer.

Just before serving, beat egg whites with remaining ½ teaspoon of vanilla and the cream of tartar to form soft peaks. Gradually add sugar, beating to form stiff peaks. Spread meringue over ice cream to edge of pie. Bake in preheated 475° oven for 4 to 5 minutes, or until meringue is browned. Serve immediately with Rum Sauce.

To Prepare Rum Sauce:
Combine all ingredients except rum. Cook and stir until mixture is thick. Stir in rum. Makes about 1 cup.

Serve the pie cut in wedges and pass the rum sauce separately.

Serves: 8

Apple-Cheese Tart

A New England favorite is hot apple pie served with slices of cheese. In California some of that cheese is baked with the apples, and the crust is a sweet pastry dough.

1½ cups all-purpose flour
7 tablespoons sugar
½ teaspoon ground cinnamon
¼ pound cold butter
2 egg yolks
2 teaspoons ice water
1 cup grated Tillamook or Cheddar Cheese
⅓ cup chopped almonds, toasted
1½ pounds tart apples, pared and thinly sliced
½ teaspoon grated lemon peel

Put flour, 3 tablespoons of sugar, and cinnamon in a bowl. Cut butter into flour mixture until it resembles fine bread crumbs. Add egg yolks and ice water and mix until the dough almost forms a ball. Press on the bottom and up the sides of a 10-inch tart pan. Chill 30 minutes. Pastry dough may also be prepared in a food processor.

Sprinkle cheese and nuts over bottom of pastry shell. Arrange apple slices over this mixture. Sprinkle with lemon peel and remaining 4 tablespoons of sugar. Bake in a preheated 400° oven for 15 minutes. Reduce heat to 350° and bake for another 20 to 25 minutes.

Serve warm with slices of Tillamook or Cheddar cheese.

Serves: 6

Glazed Artichoke Cake

6 large artichokes, cooked (or frozen artichoke hearts)
1½ cups sugar
½ cup vegetable oil
¼ cup orange juice
3 eggs
2 cups all-purpose flour
1 teaspoon baking powder
1 teaspoon baking soda
½ teaspoon grated nutmeg
½ teaspoon ground cinnamon
½ teaspoon ground ginger
½ teaspoon salt
¾ cup chopped blanched almonds
¾ cup raisins

Glaze

¼ cup orange juice
¼ cup sugar
½ teaspoon almond extract

Remove bottoms from artichokes. Clean out prickly choke and save artichoke leaves for an appetizer. Using a food processor or blender, purée artichoke bottoms. You should have 2 cups of artichoke purée.

Combine the purée with sugar, oil, orange juice, and eggs. Beat until ingredients are thoroughly blended.

Sift together flour, baking powder, baking soda, nutmeg, cinnamon, ginger, and salt. Stir into artichoke mixture, blending thoroughly. Stir in nuts and raisins, combining all ingredients.

Spoon artichoke cake mixture into a greased Bundt pan and bake in a preheated 350° oven for 1 hour.

Prepare glaze by combining orange juice, sugar, and almond extract in a saucepan. Heat until sugar has dissolved, stirring from time to time.

Remove cake from Bundt pan after it has cooled, and pour warm glaze over cake.

Yield: 1 cake

Almond Tart

¾ cup heavy cream
¾ cup sugar
¼ teaspoon salt
Juice and grated peel of 1½ lemons
⅛ teaspoon lemon extract
⅛ teaspoon almond extract
1 cup all-purpose flour
8 tablespoons butter
1 tablespoon sugar
⅛ teaspoon almond extract
1–2 tablespoons ice water
2 egg whites
½ cup almond paste
½ pound whole almonds, blanched and lightly roasted

Combine cream, ¾ cup of sugar, salt, lemon juice and peel, lemon extract, and the ⅛ teaspoon of almond extract. Mix thoroughly and reserve.

Combine flour and butter, cutting together until mixture resembles peas. Add 1 tablespoon sugar and remaining ⅛ teaspoon of almond extract. Add 1 tablespoon ice water and knead. Add more ice water if necessary until mixture forms a ball. Pastry dough may also be prepared in a food processor. Wrap pastry in waxed paper and refrigerate for 1 hour.

Roll out dough and line a 10-inch tart pan with the dough. Place in freezer for 10 minutes.

Partially bake tart shell in a preheated 400° oven for 8 minutes. Allow tart shell to cool.

Beat egg whites lightly until frothy, add almond paste, and blend thoroughly.

Spread egg white-almond paste mixture on bottom of tart. Slice toasted almonds in half, lengthwise, and stand up around edge of almond paste mixture.

Pour reserved cream mixture into tart shell. Tips of almonds will be exposed.

Place almond tart in a preheated 400°oven, and bake for 40 minutes.

Serves: 6

Dacquoise with Mocha Butter Cream
from Fournou's Ovens

6 egg whites
Pinch of salt
⅛ teaspoon cream of tartar
12 tablespoons sugar
1 teaspoon vanilla extract
⅛ teaspoon almond extract
¾ cup combined ground walnuts and hazelnuts
1 tablespoon cornstarch
3 egg yolks
1¼ cups confectioner's sugar
¾ cup milk
¾ pound butter, softened
3 tablespoons instant coffee
1 tablespoon hot water
2 tablespoons cognac
Confectioner's sugar

Beat the egg whites until they are foamy, then add salt and cream of tartar. Continue beating until soft peaks form. Slowly add 10 tablespoons of the sugar and beat until the mixture forms stiff peaks. Beat in vanilla and almond extracts.

Combine the nut mixture, cornstarch, and remaining 2 tablespoons of sugar and mix thoroughly. Fold gently into the beaten egg whites.

Draw two 10-inch circles on parchment paper and place on baking sheet. Scoop meringue mixture into a pastry bag with a ⅜-inch tip. Fill circles with the meringue and bake in the middle upper level of a preheated 300° oven for about 50 to 55 minutes, or until firm and dry. Cool to room temperature and with wide spatula remove to wire rack to cool.

Combine egg yolks and 1¼ cups confectioner's sugar and beat until thoroughly blended. Bring milk to the boiling point, pour it into the egg-sugar mixture, and blend thoroughly.

Pour egg-milk mixture into a saucepan and cook over low heat, stirring constantly, until thickened. Off heat, beat until cool. Add butter in small pieces and continue beating. When butter is completely absorbed, beat until fluffy. Dissolve instant coffee in hot water and cognac, and blend into the butter cream.

Peel the parchment paper from the meringues. Place 1 round of baked meringue on a cake platter. With a spatula, spread ⅔ of the mocha butter cream over it to within ½ inch of the edge. Put remaining cream into pastry bag with a star tip and create a decorative border around the edge of the meringue. Gently place the second meringue on top. Sprinkle with confectioner's sugar and serve at once, or refrigerate. Do not refrigerate for more than 2 hours or meringue will soften.

Serves: 8

Chocolate Decadence

1 pound dark sweet chocolate
10 tablespoons sweet butter
4 eggs
1 tablespoon sugar
1 tablespoon all-purpose flour
2 cups heavy sweet cream (whipping cream)
1 tablespoon powdered sugar
1 teaspoon vanilla extract

Cut a round of parchment paper to fit perfectly inside the bottom of an 8-inch round cake pan.

In the top of a double boiler, combine chocolate and butter. As soon as the butter and chocolate are melted, remove from the heat.

Place eggs and sugar in the top of another double boiler, and whisk until the sugar dissolves and the mixture darkens and is barely warm to the touch. Immediately remove from heat and beat at the highest speed of an electric mixer until the eggs triple in volume and are the consistency of lightly whipped cream.

Remove mixer from eggs, and fold in flour gently with a spatula.

Fold a third of the egg mixture into the chocolate mixture. Once combined, fold this chocolate mixture very gently into the remaining egg mixture.

Pour the chocolate-egg mixture into the prepared pan and tap pan lightly on the table. Bake in a preheated 400° oven for 15 minutes. Allow to cool, and place cooled cake (still in pan) in the freezer for at least a good night's rest. (Chocolate Decadence can be frozen for up to a month.)

Whip cream with powdered sugar and vanilla extract. The cream must be smooth enough to cover the cake. Do not overbeat.

Remove the Chocolate Decadence from the freezer and from its pan by momentarily spinning the pan over high heat. Turn the cake out onto a flat platter. Remove the parchment paper. Spread whipped cream on the cake. Decorate with rosettes of piped whipped cream, if you wish.

Chill, and remove from refrigerator 15 minutes before serving.

Serves: 8

After-Dinner Fig Candies

Looking for something different to serve with after-dinner espresso? Try these Hollywood favorites: fig candies. They also go very well with afternoon tea.

1 cup finely chopped dried figs (about 12–14 figs)
1¼ cups shredded coconut, finely chopped
½ cup finely chopped walnuts
2 teaspoons grated lemon peel
2 teaspoons lemon juice

Mix figs, ¾ cup of coconut, walnuts, lemon peel, and lemon juice until thoroughly combined. Using a tablespoon, press mixture into 1-inch balls. Roll candies in remaining ½ cup chopped coconut. Refrigerate for 1 hour.

Yield: 18

Holiday Fig Sweetmeats

36 dried Calimyrna figs
36 pecan halves
1 package (12 ounces) semisweet chocolate pieces
Colored sprinkles, tiny silver dragees, red or green sugar, shredded
      coconut, or chopped nuts for coating
Candy paper cups

Do not remove stems from figs. With a sharp knife, slit the bottom of each fig and press in a pecan half.

Place chocolate pieces in top of a double boiler. Stir gently until chocolate pieces are smooth and melted. Holding figs by stems, dip them halfway into the chocolate. Then dip chocolate into any of the decorative coatings. Place on a lightly oiled cookie sheet and chill until chocolate is hard. Place fig sweetmeats in small, candy paper cups before serving.

Yield: 36

Mexican-Style Dessert Coffee

¼ cup unsweetened cocoa
½ cup dark brown sugar, loosely packed
2 teaspoons ground cinnamon
4 cups water
4 tablespoons regular or percolator-grind coffee
Brandy (optional)
1 cup heavy sweet cream (whipping cream), whipped

Combine cocoa, sugar, cinnamon, and 4 cups of water in the bottom of a percolator coffee pot. Place ground coffee in the basket. Bring to a boil and perk coffee for 3 minutes.
Serve with brandy if desired, and pass a bowl of whipped cream.

Serves: 6–8

Guide to *12* California Wines

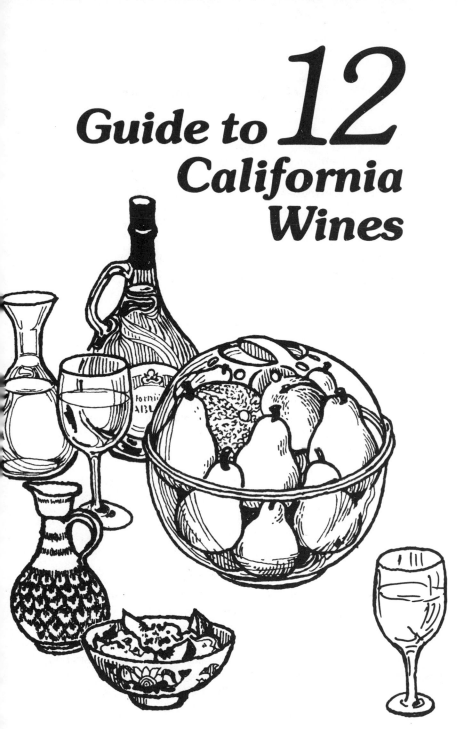

Guide to California Wines

Not too many years ago when Americans talked about wine, they talked about French, Italian, German, and other imported wines. Today, California wines have come into their own, and they're being produced in approximately 500 vineyards located in thirty-five of California's fifty-eight counties. Napa Valley, Sonoma, Mendocino, and the Lake Counties are all large wine producers, and the Santa Clara Valley proudly lays claim to producing more wine than all of them put together.

California wines are becoming more popular around the nation, and are winning blue ribbons at wine tastings where they compete against the proudest European vintages.

Some of the larger vineyards have familiar names, such as Mirassou, Beringer, Christian Brothers, Paul Masson, Robert Mondavi, and Gallo, but right alongside, and popular among the connoisseurs of California wines, are such wineries as Trefethen, Beaulieu, Lake Spring, and a large group of vineyards with "creek" in their names: Matanzas Creek, Willow Creek, Lazy Creek, Dry Creek, Conn Creek, and so on.

To drink California wines is to enter a world where new discoveries await the explorer. There are a few experts on California wines, but as yet California wines are not entrenched in the mystical lore that surrounds European wines, and the consumer need not be afraid to make decisions based on personal taste.

The choices are many, and their numbers grow constantly; so if there is confusion, it's a happy one as consumers search out the wines that most appeal to them.

The History of California Wines

The California wine industry is a mere 208 years old, young when compared to the vineyards of Europe. Father Junipero Serra and other missionaries grew grapes and made wine in settlements from San Diego to Sonoma but, according to some historians, the true father of California wine was a Hungarian, Agoston Haraszthy, who brought cuttings of Zinfandel grapes to California in 1862. Still others credit the arrival of Italians in California with the start of the wine industry, and some say that Leland Stanford, the railroad millionaire, introduced wine grapes to California in 1869.

Whoever deserves the initial credit, the vineyards of California are flourishing, and one interesting development is the increase of women holding top positions in the wineries. Zelma Long is the winemaker for Simi Vineyards, Martha Bannister and Mary Ann Graf head their own company, Vinquiry, and work as consultants to various wineries; Janet Trefethen is head of the Trefethen Vineyards, a winery that took top honors in Paris at a blind wine tasting; and Sandra Stern McIver and Merry Edwards run the Matanzas Creek Winery.

It seems that as Americans become more sure of their own tastes they drink more California wines. In 1934, California wineries shipped only 26 million gallons of wine to market; by 1960, the figure had risen to 129 million gallons, and in 1980, 314 million gallons of California wine went to the marketplace.

Quick California Takes

Champagne is among the generic wines produced in California and is presented in the familiar Champagne-type bottles. However, for those who prefer a six-pack of Champagne to a six-pack of beer at the beach, the Weibel Vineyards offers Stanford Champagne, a six-pack of Champagne with screw tops for easy opening.

This elegant six-pack is named after Leland Stanford, and, according to a Weibel marketing executive, it's the perfect beverage to serve beside the pool or after a game of tennis. The six-pack of bubbly competes in price with a six-pack of imported beer.

Types of California Wine

California table wines fall into the following categories:

Generic: As used in the United States, generic names such as Burgundy, Bordeaux, and Champagne have nothing to do with the area in which the wine is grown. California Burgundy obviously does not come from the Burgundy region of France, nor does California Champagne come from France's Champagne region. The names are used to indicate a type of wine rather than the area in which it is grown. A generic wine may be created by a blending of grapes.

Varietal: Varietal wine names are derived from the main grape variety used to make the wine: Cabernet Sauvignon, Chardonnay, Zinfandel, and so on. A varietal wine is produced mainly from the juice of a single grape variety, and if the label carries the name of the grape, the wine is a varietal.

Proprietary: A proprietary wine is a distinctive wine produced by one vineyard. It is the creation of the vintner, and is a special blend of grapes exclusive to that vineyard.

Major Varietal Wines of California

Red Wines:

Barbera

California Barbera is a descendant of the Barbera wine produced in the Piedmont region of Italy. It is dark, robust, and tartly dry with an ever-so-slightly spicy after-taste. Barbera is an excellent wine to serve with game, spicy sausage dishes, and bean casseroles.

Cabernet Sauvignon

This is one of winemaking's main red grapes, and it has been made into fine wines in Bordeaux as well as in California. The Merlot grape, which is cousin to the Cabernet Sauvignon grape, may be used in blending the wine to create a softer flavor, but many California Cabernets are made of 100% Cabernet Sauvignon grapes.

Cabernet Sauvignon wines are best when allowed to age anywhere from 3 to 10 years. They are then mellow, and have acquired a faintly herb-like tinge. Cabernet Sauvignon is excellent with beef or lamb.

Gamay

A fruity, light red wine, simple and unassuming. Gamay grapes, sometimes called Napa Gamay, are actually the true Beaujolais grapes. Gamay is excellent at informal occasions: barbecues, picnics, brunches, and lunches. It's also popular in California as a before-dinner drink, and is served chilled.

Gamay Beaujolais

Gamay Beaujolais is not really a Beaujolais grape, but is a strain of the Pinot Noir grape. Gamay Beaujolais wines are light- to medium-bodied, depending on where the vines are planted. California is currently producing a Gamay

Beaujolais in the nouveau Beaujolais style of France, and this young wine is refreshingly smooth and fruity. It is a perfect choice for brunch or a casual Sunday night supper.

Grenache

The Grenache grape is used both in rosé varietal wines, and in a blended, generic Vin Rosé. The wines made from Grenache grapes are both sweet and fruity and are especially enjoyable with rich desserts or with fruits and nuts.

Merlot

Merlot grapes are used to round out Cabernet Sauvignon wines; however Merlot wines are now becoming popular on their own, and this soft wine is especially appealing with roast birds such as squab and quail. It also goes well with cold, sliced meats.

Petite Sirah

Petite Sirah grapes were originally used in California as a blending for California Burgundy wines. However, fifteen years ago, Petite Sirah came into its own as a varietal. Petite Sirah wines are medium to full-bodied, and are a fine match with Mexican-Californian meals as well as with lamb.

Pinot Noir

Pinot Noir is a hard, cranky grape to grow. It is genetically unstable, sometimes blooming with odd variations, and is quick to come down with vineyard illnesses.

However, winemakers know that when Pinot Noir does produce properly, the resulting wine is the finest, and California winemakers do not give up easily. California Pinot Noir wines are rich with a velvety texture, and are the proper addition to dinner parties and celebrations of special occasions. Pinot Noir wines are best when aged 6 to 10 years.

Zinfandel

Zinfandel grapes are California's most widely used grapes, and there are more acres planted with Zinfandel grapes than with any other. Zinfandel wine may be consumed at all stages: a young Zinfandel is said to have a "bramble" flavor, the winemakers word for berry-like. As Zinfandel ages it develops depth and astringency, and the color becomes a dark, ruby red. When a Zinfandel has aged five years the taste of tannin is obvious, and the wine is full-bodied. Zinfandel is enjoyable with a wide variety of foods, from spicy Korean-type dishes to fruit flavored meats. It's a great companion to garlicky calzone or pizza.

White Wines:
Chardonnay or Pinot Chardonnay

This great white grape produces some of the finest white wines, and California Chardonnays have successfully met the competition of the white Burgundies of France. Some Chardonnay wines are aged in oak casks from Burgundy, and Chardonnay wines range in flavor from ripe fruitiness to a slightly tart fruitiness. Chardonnay wine may also be labeled Pinot Chardonnay, but the Chardonnay grape is not related to the Pinot grape. Chardonnay wines are memorable when served with fish dishes that have been intricately sauced or with veal dishes.

Chenin Blanc

Chenin Blanc is the popular white wine grape as Zinfandel is the popular red wine grape. Depending on the winery, Chenin Blanc is available in a variety of ways: it may be dry, medium sweet, or quite sweet. Chenin Blanc is fruity, and has been compared to the Loire Valley wines of France. A dry Chenin Blanc goes along excellently with sautéed or grilled fish, salads that contain chicken, cold turkey, and Oriental-style foods. The sweeter Chenin Blancs are companionable with fresh fruit or cooked fruit desserts.

Gewürztraminer

This is a spicy wine, with a hint of wildflowers, and it is lighter than the Gewürztraminer that comes from Alsace. Gewürztraminer is light and delicately sweet, and is excellent served as an aperitif or with the cheese course. It also complements chicken that has been prepared with a sweet sauce.

Johannisberg Riesling

California Johannisberg Riesling is made from the grapes that originally grew beside the Rhone and Mosel rivers of Germany. Johannisberg Rieslings have a wide range, and may be very dry—an excellent accompaniment to shrimp and crabmeat dishes—or may be sweet and fruity enough to be served in the afternoon with almonds or walnuts, or after dinner with dessert.

Sauvignon Blanc and Fume Blanc

Sauvignon Blanc is also known as Fume Blanc, and the *fume* is said to derive either from the smoky look of the grape at harvest time, or the smoky flavor of the grape. Sauvignon Blanc is a fresh-flavored wine, dry and versatile; it goes well with veal, seafood, chicken, and main course salads.

Minor White Wine Grapes

French Columbard grapes are used frequently in blended white jug wines and inexpensive champagnes. Pinot Blanc produces a fruity, acidy wine. Emerald Riesling and Grey Riesling yield wine that is light, slightly sweet, and has the aroma of flowers. Semillion wines are medium in body, dry, and have the bouquet of figs.

The New Light Wines:

A number of California vineyards, among them Beringer, Taylor, Sebastiani, and Paul Masson, produce wines that are somewhat lower in calories. These wines have a lower alcohol content, and as the alcohol is reduced, so are the calories. Some of these lighter-than-light wines are: Beringer's Los Hermanos Light, Sebastiani Light, Masson Light, and Taylor's Light Chablis, which contains 57 calories per glass rather than the 76 calories found in Taylor's regular Chablis.

Sophie Porter

As 13 California Goes . . . . . . So goes the nation . . . eating better every step of the way!

As California Goes . . .

Once it was Maine that seemed to influence the taste of our country. Now it's certainly California. What makes California so desirable? Why do so many people try to imitate the California way of life?

Perhaps because California offers the opportunity to create the best. According to M.F.K. Fisher, that most poetic writer about food, California offers readily available fresh foods, interesting ethnic influences, and a desire for what is natural and healthy. This, combined with a creativity and a willingness to experiment, results in new and exciting food ideas.

Lois Dwan, restaurant editor of the Los Angeles *Times,* also credits as another factor the arrival in California in recent years of many classically trained French chefs. Once away from Europe they became more inclined towards experimentation, and they adapted *cordon bleu* techniques to the endless variety of foods grown and raised in California.

But what about the *nouvelle cuisine* of France? How similar is it to California cuisine? Not similar at all, according to Andre Mercier, chef-owner of Oakland's Mirabeau restaurant, who insists that *nouvelle cuisine* is really classic French cuisine with a new name. Agreeing with him is Wolfgang Puck, owner and chef at Spago restaurant in Los Angeles. He says, "*Nouvelle cuisine* is so overcomplicated, you don't know what you're eating."

Food writer Marian Burros opined that Wolfgang Puck may be one of the links between *nouvelle cuisine* and California cuisine, serving as he does a simple dish like ravioli, but stuffing it with lobster and fresh herbs.

California cuisine is eclectic. The Hayes Street Grill in San Francisco serves a Sichuan peanut sauce over fried oysters, while the Rose and Le Favour Restaurant in St. Helena presents smoked pork tenderloin with ginger added to the traditional mustard-vinaigrette sauce. Michael's in Santa Monica serves a salad that includes tree oyster mushrooms as well as toasted pine nuts dressed with a combination of three oils, walnut, hazelnut, and olive, mixed with Cabernet Sauvignon wine vinegar.

The creative interest in food that started in California has already begun to influence the rest of the United States. More young people, many of them college graduates, are enrolling in expensive culinary academies around the country. Being a professional chef is now considered a position of prestige and glamour.

The chefs of California, while developing what seemed to be a California cuisine, have actually created the first American cuisine to cross limiting boundaries. They have combined regional American and ethnic influences while employing European cooking techniques, and they are working with the bounty of food that's produced in our country.

It's no wonder that the American Restaurant in Kansas City serves Pacific salmon and scallops in watercress sauce as well as roast peppered duck with California figs, and that the Asahi Tokyo in Long Island's Glen Cove has California Roll on its menu. When the River Cafe in Brooklyn offers dishes made with American Golden Caviar from California, can the rest of the country be far behind? Not according to the food experts who predict that the entire country will enjoy the imaginative approach to cuisine that has been pioneered in California.

Sources of
Ingredients

Sophie Porter

California Sunshine Inc.
2171 Jackson Street
San Francisco, California 94115

> American Golden Caviar
> Smoked Salmon Trout

Delegeane Garlic Farms
1518 Yountville Cross Road
Napa Valley, California 94558

> Elephant Garlic
> Regular Jumbo Garlic
> Traditional Garlic Braid
> Fresh California Bay Leaf Wreath

Marin French Cheese Company
7500 Red Hill Road
P.O. Box 99
Petaluma, California 94953

> California Rouge et Noir brand Camembert Cheese
> Breakfast Cheese
> California Rouge et Noir brand Brie Cheese
> Schloss Cheese

Wing Sing Chong Company
1076 Stockton Street
San Francisco, California 94108

> Ingredients for Chinese Cooking

Lawry's Foods, Inc.
P.O. Box 30101
Dept. GCLC
Los Angeles, California 90051

> Lawry's Products Mail Order Form
> Ingredients for California-Mexican Cooking

Williams-Sonoma
Mail Order Department—a Catalog For Cooks
P.O. Box 3792
San Francisco, California 94119

    Culinary Accessories, Ingredients, and Equipment

Ranchmen's Manufacturing
Lone Pine Ranch
P.O. Box 202029
Dallas, Texas 75220

    Mesquite wood for barbecuing

A. E. Santos
P.O. Box 1517
Laredo, Texas 78040

Star Spangled Foods
1239 Third Avenue
New York, New York 10022

    Mesquite charcoal for barbecuing

Index

A

Abalonetti's Restaurant (Monterey), 93
A. E. Santos, 179
After-Dinner Fig Candies, 163
Alice Waters's Baked Goat Cheese, 27–28
Almonds
  Fettuccine with Zucchini-Almond Sauce, 65
  Lichee Pork Chops with, 108
  Tart, 160
Amaretto, Fruit and, 42
Appetizers, 14–32, 80
  Alice Waters's Baked Goat Cheese, 27–28
  Baked Walnut Puffs, 30–31
  California Sushi Roll, 19
  Caviar Stuffed New Potatoes à la James
    Nassikas, 14
  Cheese Canapes from Buttercup Manor,
    29
  Clever California Cheese Tricks, 26
  Crab St. Jacques, 33
  Dilled Shrimp in Sour Cream, 24
  Dilly Avocado Lemon Dip, 32
  Eggplant-Olive Appetizer, 32–33
  Five O'Clock Fritters, 34
  Fried Camembert, 27
  Herb Toasted Sourdough Bread and
    Roast Peppers, 22–23
  Hot Pepper Jelly, 25
  Hummus Bi Tahini, 30
  Lemon-Marinated Mushrooms, 26
  Nutty Cheese Spread, 29–30
  Olive Pâté, 20
  Oysters in Saffron Cream Sauce, 20–21
  Pita Pocket Sandwiches, 30
  Rumaki with Figs, 16–17
  San Francisco Shrimp and Melon
    Appetizer with Sunset Dressing, 31
  Scot's Cheesecake Hors d'Oeuvre, 16
  Seeded Camembert Cheese Crisps, 28–29
  Spicy Olive-Stuffed Won Ton, 17
  Stuffed Mushrooms Delegeane, 24–25
  Tamago Sushi in the Style of
    Yamashiro, 19–20
  Tapenade, 23
  Van Nuys-Style Appetizer, 23
Apples
  -Cheese Tart, 158
  -Plum Butter, 139–40
Apricots, 54
  Homemade Preserves for Buckwheat
    Crêpes, 38
  -Vanilla Chantilly, 42
  Yogurt Dessert, 144
Artichokes, 54
  Blackeye Peas and Artichoke Heart
    Salad, 71
  Corn and Artichoke Chili Bonanza,
    56–57
  Crab-Stuffed, 87
  Cream of Artichoke Soup, 46–47
  Easy Cream of Artichoke Soup, 46–47
  Glazed Artichoke Cake, 159

Monterey Artichokes with Shrimp and
    Lemon Sauce, 91
  'n Hot Corn, 57
Avocado, 54
  Dilly Avocado Lemon Dip, 32
  Dips for Raw Vegetables, 61
  Filled Avocado, 42
  Guacamole I, 68
  Guacamole II, 68–69
  Mushroom Salad in, 70
  Richard Condon's Guacamole, 69

B

Baked Fig Pudding and Sauce, 151
Baked Figs in Wine, 43
Baked Fish Fillets with Clams and
    Grapes, 76
Baked Praline Ice Cream Pie with Rum
    Sauce, 157–58
Baked Walnut Puffs, 30–31
Balboa Cafe, 22, 84
Barbecue
  Korean Beef, 99
  Sauce St. Helena, 132
Barbera Wine, 168
Batori, Ron, 15
Beans, 55
  Beef Chimichangas, 98
  Cowboy Bean and Ham Stew, 108
  Santa Ynez Valley Bean and Chili
    Soup, 47
Beef
  Braised Beef Ribs Korean, 100
  Chimichangas, 98
  Flank Steak with Pears, 102
  Jeff's Carne Asado Burrito Brunch, 40
  Korean Beef Barbecue, 99
  Sacramento Stuffed Steak, 103
  Slivered Steak Tartare from Korea,
    100–101
  Smoked Brisket of, 41
Beringer Vineyards, 15–16
Beringer Vineyards Tomato Chicken
    Soup, 51–52
Blackeye Peas and Artichoke Heart
    Salad, 71
Bouillabaisse West Coast Style, 94
Braised Beef Ribs Korean, 100
Bread, 44
  Garlic Toast, 101
  Green Chili Spoon, 126–27
  Herb Toasted Sourdough Bread and
    Roast Peppers, 22–23
  Olive Onion, 126
  San Francisco's Sourdough, 124–25
Broiled Tuna Steak with Orange
    Butter à la Jeremiah Tower, 85
Brunch, 9–10, 35–44
  Apricot-Vanilla Chantilly, 42
  Baked Figs in Wine, 43
  Buckwheat Crêpes with Caviar, 37–38
  Crab and Vegetable Omelet, 38–39

Filled Avocado, 42
Frontier Flapjacks with Prune Sauce,
    40–41
Frozen Peach Dessert, 43
Fruit and Amaretto, 42
Homemade Apricot Preserves for
    Buckwheat Crêpes, 38
Jeff's Carne Asado Burrito Brunch, 40
Smoked Brisket of Beef, 41
Stacked Ricotta Pancakes with Fruit, 37
Sunflower Tuna Muffin, 42
Thirty-Minute Ham and Fig Brunch for
    Two, 39
Tomato-Olive Sorbet, 36
Buckwheat Crêpes with Caviar, 37–38
Burritos, 130
Jeff's Carne Asado Burrito Brunch, 40
Burros, Marian, 174
Butter
    Apple-Plum, 139–40
    Clarified, 106
    Flavored, 133
    Garlic, 92
    Prune, 140

C

Cabbage and Nuts, 59
Cabernet Sauvignon Wine, 168
Cake, Glazed Artichoke, 159
California Champagne Sorbet, 142–43
California Cuisine
    and nouvelle cuisine, 48–50, 174
    Base of, 54
    Defined, 4–5, 15, 21, 174–75
    Development of regional cuisine, 15–16
California Culinary Academy, 15
California Sunshine, 88–89, 178
California Sushi Roll, 19
Calzone from Café Chez Panisse, 128–29
Candy
    After-Dinner Fig Candies, 163
Cantaloupe Sorbet, 142
Caramelized Mandarin Oranges, 152–53
Carrots
    Cream of Carrot and Tomato Soup, 48
Caviar
    Buckwheat Crêpes with, 37–38
    Stuffed New Potatoes à la James
        Nassikas, 14
    Also see Golden Caviar.
Chalupa, 107
Champagne, California Sorbet, 142–43
Chardonnay Wine, 170
Cheese
    Alice Waters's Baked Goat, 27–28
    Apple-Cheese Tart, 158
    Canapes from Buttercup Manor, 29
    Clever California Tricks, 26
    Five O'Clock Fritters, 34
    Fried Camembert, 27
    Nutty Cheese Spread, 29–30
    Parmesan Dressing, 70

Seeded Camembert Cheese Crisps, 28–29
Stacked Ricotta Pancakes with Fruit, 37
-Stuffed Squab, Scot Horrobin Style,
    119–20
Cheesecake
    Scot's Cheesecake Hors d'Oeuvre, 15
Cheese Canapes from Buttercup Manor, 29
Chenin Blanc Wine, 170
Chez Panisse (Berkeley), 21–22, 26, 63,
    84, 89, 128–29
Chicken
    Beringer Vineyards Tomato Chicken
        Soup, 51–52
    Cheese-Stuffed Squab, Scot Horrobin
        Style, 119–20
    Roast Chicken with Garlic Sauce, 115
    Roast Squab, 118–19
    Roast Squab Chickens Stuffed with
        Figs and Olives, 117–18
    San Francisco Style Chinese Chicken
        Salad, 115–16
    Spiced Chicken Breasts with Grapes,
        116–17
    Squab Soong, Mandarin Style, 120–21
Chili
    Corn and Artichoke Bonanza, 56–57
    Green Chili Spoon Bread, 126–27
    Olive and Chili Pie, 128
    Santa Ynez Valley Bean and Chili
        Soup, 47
Chocolate
    Decadence, 162–63
    Dipped Fruits, 150–51
Clafouti
    Grape, 145–46
    Peach, 145
Clams
    Baked Fish Fillets with Clams and
        Grapes, 76
Clever California Cheese Tricks, 26
Coffee, Mexican-Style Dessert, 164
Cold Lemon Mousse in the Style of
    Fournou's Ovens, 147–48
Corn
    and Artichoke Chili Bonanza, 56–57
    Artichoke 'n Hot, 57
Cowboy Bean and Ham Stew, 108
Crab
    and Vegetable Omelet, 38–39
    and Vegetables Orientale, 88
    St. Jacques, 33
    -Stuffed Artichokes, 87
Crème Fraîche, 60
Crêpes
    Buckwheat with Caviar, 37–38
    Seafood, 90–91
Cream of Artichoke Soup with Crushed
    Hazelnuts, 46–47
Cream of Carrot and Tomato Soup, 48
Cream of Lettuce Soup, 50
Curry
    Shrimp Curry Pacifica, 91–92
    Vegetarian, 58

D

Dacquoise with Mocha Butter Cream
   from Fournou's Ovens, 161–62
Date Shake, 155
Delegeane Garlic Farms, 114, 178
Delegeane, Jim, 114
Delegeane, Nyda, 81, 114
Desserts, 142–64
   After-Dinner Fig Candies, 163
   Almond Tart, 160–61
   Apple-Cheese Tart, 158
   Apricot Yogurt Dessert, 144
   Baked Fig Pudding and Sauce, 151
   Baked Praline Ice Cream Pie with Rum
     Sauce, 157–58
   California Champagne Sorbet, 142–43
   Cantaloupe Sorbet, 142
   Caramelized Mandarin Oranges, 152–53
   Chocolate Decadance, 162–63
   Chocolate Dipped Fruits, 150–51
   Cold Lemon Mousse in the Style of
     Fournou's Ovens, 147–48
   Dacquoise with Mocha Butter Cream from
     Fournou's Ovens, 161–62
   Date Shake, 155
   Fresh Fruit Sorbet, 143
   Fresh Persimmon and Fig Dessert, 154
   Fresh Raspberry Sorbet, 144
   Frozen Peach Mousse, 148
   Glazed Artichoke Cake, 159
   Grape Clafouti, 145–46
   Holiday Fig Sweetmeats, 163
   Hot Prune Puffs, 155
   Lemon Granita, 143–44
   Light Raspberry Soufflé, 148
   Macaroon Cream, 150
   Mexican-Style Dessert Coffee, 164
   Oranges in Red Wine, 152
   Peach Clafouti, 145
   Pears Caramel, 153
   Stuffed Pears in Red Wine, 154
   Sugared Grape Clusters, 151–52
   Tortilla Flats as Served at Lawry's
     California Center, 156–57
   Wine-Grape Dessert, 149–50
Dilled Shrimp in Sour Cream, 24
Dilly Avocado Lemon Dip, 32
Dips for Raw Vegetables, 61
Dreyfus, Raymond, 149
Dwan, Lois, 174

E

Easy Cream of Artichoke Soup, 46–47
Eggplant-Olive Appetizer, 32–33
Elephant Garlic, 5, 114–15
   Roast Chicken with Garlic Sauce, 115
   Stuffed Mushrooms Delegeane, 24–25
Engstrom, Mats and Dafne, 88–89

F

Fettuccine with Zucchini-Almond Sauce, 65
Figs, 55
   After-Dinner Fig Candies, 163

Baked Fig Pudding and Sauce, 151
Baked, in Wine, 43
California Pickled, 138–39
Chutney, 138
Fresh Persimmon and Fig Dessert, 154
Holiday Fig Sweetmeats, 163–64
Lamb Kebabs with, 102
Roast Squab Chickens Stuffed with Figs
   and Olives, 117–18
Rumaki with, 16–17
Thirty-Minute Ham and Fig Brunch for
   Two, 39
Fish
   Baked Fish Fillets with Clams and
     Grapes, 76
   Bouillabaisse West Coast Style, 94
   Broiled Tuna Steaks with Orange Butter
     à la Jeremiah Tower, 85
   Fisherman's Wharf Fish Stew, 95
   Fresno Baked Fish Fillets, 75–76
   Halibut with Walnuts in Foil, 77–78
   Mirassou Vineyards Seafood Terrine,
     80–81
   Phil Paladino's Quick Ziti and Tuna, 86
   Salmon Sausalito, 79
   Salmon Steaks with Garlic Confit, 78–79
   Sunflower Tuna Muffiin, 42
   Tacos, 76–77
   Truite en Chemise à la Restaurant
     L'Escoffier, 83–84
   Van Nuys-Style Appetizer, 23
   Also see Shellfish.
Fish Tacos, 76–77
Fisher, M.F.K., 174
Fisherman's Wharf Fish Stew, 95
Five O'Clock Fritters, 34
Flank Steak with Pears, 102
Fresh Fruit Sorbet, 143
Fresh Peaches and Sausage, 111
Fresh Persimmon and Fig Dessert, 154
Fresh Raspberry Sorbet, 144
Fresno Baked Fish Fillets, 75–76
Fried Camembert, 27
Frontier Flapjacks with Prune Sauce, 40–41
Frozen Peach Dessert, 43
Frozen Peach Mousse, 148
Fruit
   A West Coast Pretty, 39
   and Amaretto, 42
   Chocolate Dipped, 150–51
   Fresh Fruit Sorbet, 143
   Stacked Ricotta Pancakes with, 37
   Stir-Fried Vegetables and, 61
   Also see individual fruits.
Fume Blanc Wine, 171

G

Gamay Beaujolais Wine, 168–69
Gamay Wine, 168
Garlic
   Elephant, 5, 114–15
   Hot Garlic-Anchovy Sauce, 133
   Roast Chicken with Garlic Sauce, 115
   Salmon Steaks with Garlic Confit, 78–79

Salt, 101
Shrimp with Garlic Butter, 92
Toast, 101
Vegetable Quiche in Garlic Crust,
    127–28
Gewürztraminer Wine, 170
Glazed Artichoke Cake, 159
Golden Caviar
    Buckwheat Crêpes with, 37–38
    Developed, 88–89
    Sauce, 132
    Spinach Pasta & Scallops with, 89–90
    Stuffed New Potatoes à la James
        Nassikas, 14
Granola, Grapes 'n, 39
Grapes, 55
    and Leek Sauce with Wine, 133–34
    Baked Fish Fillets with Clams and, 76
    Clafouti, 145
    Kiwi-Grape Sauce, 136–37
    'n Granola, 39
    Spiced Chicken Breasts with, 116–17
    Sugared Clusters, 151–52
    Wine-Grape Dessert, 149–50
Green Chili Spoon Bread, 126–27
Green Salsa Mexicana I, 134
Green's restaurant at Ft. Mason
    (San Francisco), 22, 26, 62–64
Grenache Wine, 169
Guacamole
    I, 68
    II, 68–69
    Richard Condon's, 69

H

Halibut with Walnuts in Foil, 77–78
Ham
    Cowboy Bean and Ham Stew, 108
    Kiwi Fruit with Prosciutto, 24
    Thirty-Minute Ham and Fig Brunch for
        Two, 39
Herb Toasted Sourdough Bread and Roast
    Peppers, 22–23
Holiday Fig Sweetmeats, 163–64
Homemade Apricot Preserves for Buckwheat
    Crêpes, 38
Horrobin, Scot, 15–16
    Cheese-Stuffed Squab, Scot Horrobin
        Style, 118–19
Hot Garlic-Anchovy Sauce, 133
Hot Pepper Jelly, 25
Hot Prune Puffs, 155
Hummus Bi Tahini, 30

I

Ice Cream
    Apricot-Vanilla Chantilly, 42
    Baked Praline Ice Cream Pie and Rum
        Sauce, 157–58

J

Jeff's Carne Asado Burrito Brunch, 40
Jim's Skordalia Sauce or Spread, 137

Johannisberg Riesling Wine, 170–71
Joseph Phelps Winery, 15

K

Kiwi Fruit, 55, 80, 103
    -Grape Sauce, 136–37
    Lamb with Kiwi Fruit Sauce, 103–104
    Sage-Flavored Pork Chops with, 109
    with Prosciutto Ham, 24
Korean Beef Barbecue, 6
Korean Cuisine California Style, 99–101

L

L'Escoffier (Beverly Hills), 26, 82–83,
    149
Lamb
    in Mushroom Cream Sauce, 104–105
    Kebabs with Figs, 102
    Plum Sauce for, 136
    Rack of, with Sauce Paloise, 105–106
    Sonoma County Spice-Cured Rack of,
        106–107
    with Kiwi Fruit Sauce, 103–104
Lawry's California Center, 156
Lawry's Foods, Inc., 178
Lemon
    Cold Lemon Mousse in the Style of
        Fournou's Ovens, 147–48
    Granita, 143–44
    -Marinated Mushrooms, 26
Lettuce, Cream of, Soup, 50
Lichee Pork Chops with Almonds, 108–109
Light Raspberry Soufflé, 149
Light Wines of California, 171

M

Ma Maison (Los Angeles), 89
Macaroon Cream, 150
Madison, Deborah, 22, 63
Mahler, Richard, 15
Mandarin restaurant (San Francisco), 120
Marin French Cheese Company, 178
Marinated Tofu and Vegetables on Skewers
    in the Manner of Green's restaurant in
    San Francisco, 64–65
Meat, 97–122. *Also see* Beef, Lamb,
    Pork, Veal.
Melon
    San Francisco Shrimp and Melon
        Appetizer with Sunset Dressing, 31
Mercier, Andre, 48–50, 174
Merlot Wine, 169
Mexican-Style Dessert Coffee, 164
Michael's (Los Angeles), 89
Mirabeau Restaurant (Oakland), 48, 174
Mirassou Vineyards Seafood Terrine, 80–81
Mirassou Winery, 48
Monterey Artichokes with Shrimp and
    Lemon Sauce, 91
Mousse
    Cold Lemon, in the Style of Fournou's
        Ovens, 147–48
    Frozen Peach, 149

Mushrooms
  Lamb in Mushroom Cream Sauce,
    104–105
  Lemon-Marinated, 26
  Salad in Avocado, 70
  -Spinach Salad with Almonds in Parmesan
    Dressing, 70
  Stuffed Mushrooms Delegeane, 24–25

N

Napa Valley, 15
Napa Valley Relish, 139
Nassikas, James, 14, 146–47
Nectarines, 55–56
  -Tomato Refresher, 51
Norris, Christopher, 41
Nuts
  Almond Tart, 160
  Baked Walnut Puffs, 30–31
  Cabbage and, 59
  Cream of Artichoke Soup with Crushed
    Hazelnuts, 46
  Dacquoise with Mocha Butter Cream from
    Fournou's Ovens, 161–62
  Halibut with Walnuts in Foil, 77–78
  Lichee Pork Chops with Almonds, 108
  Walnut Sauce and Leftover Turkey, 122
Nutty Cheese Spread, 29–30
Nyda's Snapper and Spinach, 81–82

O

Olives, 55
  and Chili Pie, 128
  Eggplant-Olive Appetizer, 32–33
  Onion Bread, 126
  Pâté, 20
  Roast Squab Chickens Stuffed with Figs
    and, 117–18
  Spicy Olive-Stuffed Won Ton, 17
  Tomato-Olive Sorbet, 36
Omelet, Crab and Vegetable, 38–39
Onions, and Olive Bread, 126
Orange Peel, 111
Oranges, 58
  Caramelized Mandarin, 152–53
  in Red Wine, 152
Oysters in Saffron Cream Sauce, 20–21

P

Pancakes
  Buckwheat Crêpes with Caviar, 37
  Frontier Flapjacks with Prune Sauce,
    40–41
  Stacked Ricotta Pancakes with Fruit, 37
Papaya
  Baked, 137
  Teatime Spread, 138
Parmesan Dressing, 70
Party Menus, 9–11
Party Themes, 10–11
Pasta
  Fettuccine with Zucchini-Almond Sauce, 65

Phil Paladino's Quick Ziti and Tuna, 86
Spinach Pasta & Scallops with Golden
    Caviar, 89–90
Pâté
  Olive, 20
  Vegetable, 59–60
Peaches, 56
  Clafouti, 145
  Fresh Peaches and Sausage, 111
  Frozen Dessert, 43
  Frozen Mousse, 148
Pears, 55
  Caramel, 153
  Flank Steak with, 102
  Salmon Sausalito, 79
  Stuffed in Red Wine, 154
Peppers
  Herb Toasted Sourdough Bread and
    Roast, 22–23
  Hot Pepper Jelly, 25
Persimmon
  Fresh Persimmon and Fig Dessert, 154
Petite Sirah Wine, 169
Phil Paladino's Quick Ziti and Tuna, 86
Pie
  Baked Praline Ice Cream with Rum
    Sauce, 157–58
  Olive and Chili, 128
Pinot Chardonnay Wine, 170
Pinot Noir Wine, 169
Pita Pocket Sandwiches, 30
Plums, 56
  Apple-Plum Butter, 139–40
  Sauce for Roast Pork or Lamb, 136
  Tabouli with, 62
Polenta, Marin County and Sausage, 112
Pork
  Chalupa, 107
  Cowboy Bean and Ham Stew, 108
  Fresh Peaches and Sausage, 111
  Lichee Pork Chops with Almonds,
    108–109
  Marin County Polenta and Sausage, 112
  Plum Sauce for, 136
  Sage-Flavored Pork Chops with Kiwi Fruit
    Sauce, 109
  Tofu-Pork Balls Rong Shing Style, 110
Potatoes, Caviar Stuffed New, à la James
    Nassikas, 14
Poultry. *See* Chicken, Turkey.
Preserves, Apricot, Homemade, for
    Buckwheat Crêpes, 38
Prunes, 56
  Butter, 140
  Frontier Flapjacks with Prune Sauce,
    40–41
  Hot Prune Puffs, 155
Puck, Wolfgang, 174

Q

Quiche, Vegetable in Garlic Crust,
    127–28

R

Ranchmen's Manufacturing, 179
Raspberry
    Fresh Sorbet, 144
    Light Soufflé, 149
Red Wines of California, 168–70
Relishes
    California Pickled Figs, 138–39
    Fig Chutney, 138
    Napa Valley Relish, 139
Roast Chicken with Garlic Sauce, 115
Roast Squab, 118–19
Roast Squab Chickens Stuffed with Figs
    and Olives, 117–18
Rum Sauce, 157, 158
Rumaki with Figs, 16–17
Rutherford Hill Winery, 15

S

Sacramento Stuffed Steak, 103
Sage-Flavored Pork Chops with Kiwi Fruit
    Sauce, 109
Salads
    Blackeye Peas and Artichoke Heart, 71
    Mushroom in Avocado, 70
    Mushroom-Spinach with Almonds in
        Parmesan Dressing, 70
Salmon
    Sausalito, 79
    Steaks with Garlic Confit, 78–79
Salsa Mexicana II, 135
Salsa Mexicana III, 135
Salt, Garlic, 101
San Francisco Shrimp and Melon Appetizer
    with Sunset Dressing, 31
San Francisco Style Chinese Chicken
    Salad, 115–16
San Francisco's Sourdough Bread, 22,
    124–25
Sandwiches
    Burrito, 130
    Pita Pocket, 30
Sangria, 9, 10
Santa Ynez Valley Bean and Chili Soup, 47
Sauces
    Barbecue Sauce St. Helena, 132
    Golden Caviar, 132
    Grape and Leek Sauce with Wine, 133–34
    Green Salsa Mexicana I, 134
    Hot Garlic-Anchovy, 133
    Jim's Skordalia Sauce or Spread, 137
    Kiwi-Grape Sauce, 136–37
    Plum Sauce for Roast Pork or Lamb, 136
    Rum, 157, 158
    Salsa Mexicana II, 135
    Salsa Mexicana III, 135
    Sauce Louis, 135–36
    Sauce Paloise, 105–106
    Sauce Verte, 81
Sausage
    Fresh Peaches and, 111
    Marin County Polenta and, 112

Sauvignon Blanc Wine, 171
Scallops
    Spinach Pasta & Scallops with Golden
        Caviar, 89–90
Scalloppine of Veal with Mustard, 112–13
Scalloppine with Lemon Sauce
    à La Stanford Court, 113
Scot's Cheesecake Hors d'Oeuvre, 16
Seafood Crêpes, 90–91
Seeded Camembert Cheese Crisps, 28–29
Shellfish
    Baked Fish Fillets with Clams and
        Grapes, 76
    Bouillabaisse West Coast Style, 94
    Crab and Vegetable Omelet, 38–39
    Crab and Vegetables Orientale, 88
    Crab St. Jacques, 33
    Crab-Stuffed Artichokes, 87
    Dilled Shrimp in Sour Cream, 24
    Fisherman's Wharf Fish Stew, 95
    Mirassou Vineyards Seafood Terrine,
        80–81
    Monterey Artichokes with Shrimp and
        Lemon Sauce, 91
    San Francisco Shrimp and Melon
        Appetizer with Sunset Dressing, 31
    Seafood Crêpes, 90–91
    Shrimp and Kiwi Fruit, 80
    Shrimp and Curry Pacifica, 91–92
    Shrimp with Garlic Butter, 92
    Spinach Pasta & Scallops with Golden
        Caviar, 89–90
    Squid Abalonetti, 93
Shrimp
    Dilled Shrimp in Sour Cream, 24
    Monterey Artichokes with Shrimp and
        Lemon Sauce, 91
    Pacifica Curry, 91–92
    San Francisco Shrimp and Melon
        Appetizer with Sunset Dressing, 31
    Seafood Crêpes, 90–91
    with Garlic Butter, 92
Slivered Steak Tartare from Korea, 100–101
Smoked Brisket of Beef, 41
Sonoma County Spice-Cured Rack of Lamb,
    106–107
Sorbet
    California Champagne, 142–43
    Cantaloupe, 142
    Fresh Fruit, 143
    Fresh Raspberry, 144
    Tomato-Olive, 36
Soufflé, Light Raspberry, 149
Soups, 45–52
    Beringer Vineyards Tomato Chicken,
        51–52
    Bouillabaisse West Coast Style, 94
    Cream of Artichoke with Crushed
        Hazelnuts, 46
    Cream of Carrot and Tomato, 48
    Cream of Lettuce, 50
    Easy Cream of Artichoke, 46–47
    Fisherman's Wharf Fish Stew, 95

Nectarine-Tomato Refresher, 51
Santa Ynez Valley Bean and Chili, 47
Turkey Tortilla, 52
Sourdough Starter, 124–25
Spiced Chicken Breasts with Grapes, 116–17
Spicy Olive-Stuffed Won Ton, 17
Spinach
    Mushroom-Spinach Salad with Almonds in
        Parmesan Dressing, 70
    Nyda's Snapper and Spinach, 81–82
    Truit en Chemise à la Restaurant
        L'Escoffier, 83–84
    Spinach Pasta & Scallops with Golden
        Caviar, 89–90
Squab Chickens
    Cheese-Stuffed Squab, Scot Horrobin
        Style, 119–20
    Roast Squab, 118–19
    Roasted and Stuffed with Figs and
        Olives, 117–18
    Soong, Mandarin Style, 120–21
Squid Abalonetti, 93
Stacked Ricotta Pancakes with Fruit, 37
Stanford Court Hotel (San Francisco),
    14, 89, 146–47
Star Spangled Foods, 179
Stew
    Cowboy Bean and Ham Stew, 108
    Fisherman's Wharf Fish Stew, 95
Stuffed Mushrooms Delegeane, 24–25
Stuffed Pears in Red Wine, 154
Sugared Grape Clusters, 151–52
Sunflower Tuna Muffin, 42
Sushi, 18–20
    California Roll, 19
    Tamago Sushi in the Style of
        Yamashiro, 19–20

T

Tabouli with Plums, 62
Tacos, Fish, 76–77
Tamago Sushi in the Style of Yamashiro,
    19–20
Tangerines, 58
Tapenade, 23
Tart, Almond, 160
Thirty-Minute Ham and Fig Brunch for Two,
    39
Tofu
    Marinated Tofu and Vegetables on
        Skewers in the Manner of Green's
        restaurant in San Francisco, 64–65
    -Pork Balls Rong Shing Style, 110
Tomato
    Beringer Vineyards Tomato Chicken
        Soup, 51–52
    Cream of Carrot and Tomato Soup, 48
    Nectarine-Tomato Refresher, 51
    Sun-Dried as Appetizers, 28

Tomato-Olive Sorbet, 36
Tortillas
    Tortilla Flats as Served at Lawry's
        California Center, 156–57
    Turkey Tortilla Soup, 52
Tower, Jeremiah, 22, 84–85
Trefethen Winery, 15
Truite en Chemise à la Restaurant
        L'Escoffier, 83–84
Tuna
    Broiled Tuna Steaks with Orange Butter
        à la Jeremiah Tower, 85
    Phil Paladino's Quick Ziti and, 86
    Sunflower Tuna Muffin, 42
Turkey
    Cutlets Cantonese, 121–22
    Tortilla Soup, 52
    Walnut Sauce and Leftover, 122

V

Van Nuys-Style Appetizer, 23
Veal
    Scalloppine with Lemon Sauce à
        La Stanford Court, 113
    Scalloppine with Mustard, 112–13
Vegetables, 53–71
    Crab and Vegetable Omelet, 38–39
    Crab and Vegetables Orientale, 88
    Dips for, 61
    Pâté, 59–60
    Quiche in Garlic Crust, 127–28
    Stir-Fried and Fruit, 61
    Also see specific vegetables.
Vegetarian Curry, 58

W

Walnuts
    Halibut with Walnuts in Foil, 77–78
    Sauce and Leftover Turkey, 122
Waters, Alice, 21–22, 26, 27, 63, 84, 128
West Coast Pretty, 39
White Wines of California, 170–71
Williams-Sonoma, 3, 179
Wine-Grape Dessert, 149–50
Wines of California, 165–71
Wing Sing Chong Company, 178
Won Ton, Spicy Olive-Stuffed, 17

Y

Yamashiro's (Hollywood), 18–20
Yogurt, Apricot, Dessert, 144

Z

Zinfandel Wine, 169–70
Ziti, Phil Paladino's Quick, and Tuna, 86
Zucchini
    Fettuccine with Zucchini-Almond Sauce, 65
    Napa Valley Relish, 139